FUNNY SHORTS 2

TEN MORE COMIC PLAYS

VOLUME 2

Copyright © 2021 by John McDonnell

All rights reserved. This book or any portion thereof may not be reproduced or used in any manner whatsoever without the express written permission of the publisher except for the use of brief quotations in a book review.

Printed in the United States of America
First Printing, 2021
ISBN 9798511790091

John McDonnell Publishing
39 Doyle Street
Doylestown, PA 18901
www.johnfmcdonnell.com

WHAT THEY'RE SAYING ABOUT *FUNNY SHORTS*...

As a master of the short play form, John McDonnell holds up a mirror to the way we live now. Always revealing, always spot on, and always very funny, his plays are a dream for actors. Easy to produce -- they work as well on a bare stage as they do in a fully realized production. Either way, the audiences are always entertained and leave the theatre happier than when they came in. You will enjoy reading or performing the works of John McDonnell.

—John Augustine is a playwright, television writer, actor and director. He has taught playwriting in New York City at Playwrights Horizons Theatre School, The 42nd Street Collective, NYU, and at Sarah Lawrence College.

Every theatre instructor needs that absolutely infallible book of scenes for students. John McDonnell's plays are full of hilarious reveals and quirky character studies, with plot twists that provide actors with meaningful discussion about motivation, foreshadowing, and bold choices.

What's even better? The length of the comic short plays provides significant opportunities for memorization and stage time for everyone involved. This is the perfect comedy collection for your studio classroom!

—Sarah LeClair is the Youth Education Director at Comedy Sportz Philadelphia and a curriculum writer/consultant for The Philadelphia Shakespeare Theatre teaching artist program. Sarah has spent more than twenty years in new play development and performing arts opportunities for community theatres, undergraduate college programs, and high school actors.

John finds the absurd in the mundane, the fracture in the fable. Guaranteed a laugh in every bite!

—Joey Perillo calls himself an erstwhile cab driver, but in reality he's a veteran character actor who has appeared as a principal (speaking) actor in virtually every theatrical medium, including 14 major motion pictures (*Philadelphia*, *12 Monkeys*, *Rachel Getting Married*, *The Negotiator*,** and ***The Manchurian Candidate*,** **among others), and the original (and best)** *Hairspray*. **He has also appeared as a principal on TV shows like** *ER*, *Hack*, *Homicide*, *The Wire*, **and** *The Sopranos*. **Joey**

is a long-time member of the Screen Actors Guild and Actors Equity Association.

It's always an honor to work with John McDonnell, and I've been fortunate to perform many of his short plays. They are always witty, engaging, and relatable. John creates likable characters and gives them dialogue that makes the audience think about the human condition in a hysterical way.

—Dave Levy is an educator, actor, and comedic improvisor. He is the Director of the Summer Youth Workshops at Town and Country Players, Buckingham PA, and has performed in 12 shows at T&C in recent years. In addition, Dave has been involved with New Feathers Productions, Playwright's Bridge workshop group, and Funny Shorts. He is an active performer in a comedic improv troupe called Bucket of Phones.

McDonnell's genius lies in putting his quirky characters into ordinary scenarios and then letting us watch how they react when circumstances go seriously awry. The men and women he gives life to in his plays are both warm and wacky, the kind of people I would love to get to know at a party. He peoples his stories with individuals who consistently refuse to do the expected.

—Author Lisa DeAngelis's *Angels Unaware* will be published by Regal House in June, 2021.

John's plays are warm, funny, and heartfelt. They are fun to perform because each character has a very strong objective right from the start. I find an inherent goodness and hope in his writing.

—**Righteous Jolly is a Circle In The Square Alumnus (2003). His regional credits include:** *Sweeney Todd, Jesus Christ Superstar, Orphans* **(Phillip),** *Marvin's Room* **(Hank),** *Mirette* **(Bellini)** *Bloody Bloody Andrew Jackson* **(Andrew Jackson),** *Mamma Mia* **(Sam Carmichael). Film, TV, & Web: Robert McKenzie in** *Gemini Rising***. Krampus in** *Merry Krampus***. Lorenzo de Medici and King Charlemagne in** *The Pope: A Mini Series***.**

INTRODUCTION

This is my second book of funny plays. I published *Funny Shorts Volume 1* in January of 2021, in the middle of the COVID-19 global pandemic, which didn't seem like the best time to publish a book of humorous plays.

After all, the world seemed a pretty grim place in those days. The news headlines were very discouraging. Many people had gotten sick, the number of deaths was increasing, and the future didn't look particularly promising.

Who's interested in laughing at a time like that?

It turns out a lot of people were. *Funny Shorts* sold very well, and it's still selling briskly. I think it's because people needed some relief from those awful news headlines, and it felt good for them to read my plays and laugh their troubles away.

Humor has always been the best remedy for gloomy news, I believe. There's nothing better than a good laugh to make you forget your troubles. Just writing these plays lifts my spirits, and seeing the reaction when they're performed tells me they lift the spirits of an audience too.

So here is *Funny Shorts Volume 2*, another collection of short, funny plays. Most of them have been performed or read in front of audiences all over the US. I guarantee there are a few laughs here for you, even if you're just reading them in the privacy of your home.

And after you stop laughing, you might just decide you want to see them performed.

Which is great! My plays are perfect for performances, whether in person or through livestreaming, on a podcast, an audio play, or other venues. There are no rigid requirements about costumes, sets, lighting, or anything else. The dialogue is not complicated, and there are no physical demands on the actors.

These plays work well for student drama classes or productions, community theaters, senior centers – really, just about any type of production you can think of.

Want to put my plays on? My fee is reasonable -- $20 for each play. I charge the $20 fee for performance rights to each play up to five, and $60 for a group of six plays or more. Just email me at mcdonnellwrite@gmail.com and we'll work out the details. By the way, that's a one-time permission: if you're interested in the rights to multiple performances, email me for more information.

Note: Even with my permission you must credit me as the author in any advertising or promotional material. I'll be happy to promote your performance on my social media if you give me the details. If you need a PDF copy of the plays for your actors, let me know and I'll send it to you for a fee of $20 per play. All you need to do is send me an email – mcdonnellwrite@gmail.com.

PLEASE UNDERSTAND, I AM NOT GIVING PERMISSION FOR ANYONE TO REPRINT MY PLAYS, PUBLISH THEM FOR SALE IN ANY FORMAT, OR SELL VIDEO OR AUDIO RECORDINGS OF THEM.

If you have any questions, comments, or suggestions, let me know. And by the way, I LOVE getting feedback on my plays! By all means, let me know what your audience thinks.

Thank you for buying a copy of *Funny Shorts Volume 2*. I know you're going to get a good laugh from these plays.

And that's something we all need these days!

John McDonnell

PUBLISHER STATEMENT

FICTITIOUS DISCLAIMER

This book is a work of fiction. Any similarity between the characters and situations within its pages and places or persons, living or dead, is unintentional and co-incidental.

DEDICATION

To my wife Anita. Thanks for all the laughter.

Table of Contents

Love Bite	1
Grilling Whitey	21
Love You Madly	39
Candy Heart	58
A Kiss In Time	81
Are You Happy?	105
Game Theory	122
Less Is More	134
How To Spot A Zombie	151
Recovered Memory	168

LOVE BITE

FUNNY SHORTS 2

CHARACTERS

VICKY   Fortyish, dressed for a date. Speaks fast because of her nervousness. Is very self-absorbed.

DRACULA   Eternally fiftyish. Dark hair, pale skin. He is wearing a cape. He has an Eastern European accent, and pronounces "W" as "V", and vice versa. He also pronounces laboratory this way: la-BORE—atory. He speaks slowly and has an overly dignified air, but also with an air of melodrama, like Bela Lugosi, who played Dracula in the old movies.

WAITRESS   Can be any age from 20-60. She chews gum and has a sassy attitude.

FUNNY SHORTS 2

SETTING

A restaurant. Vicky is sitting at a table when Dracula enters.

TIME

Early evening.

Dracula enters and walks up to Vicky's table.

DRACULA
Good evening. *(bowing)* Are you Victoria?

VICKY
Are you Vlad? That's just your screen name, right? It's such an unusual name! You don't meet many Vlads these days.

DRACULA
He bows again

I am pleased to meet you, Victoria.

VICKY
No need to get all formal here – I'm just plain old Vicky, you don't have to be a tight ass around me. Have a seat, Vladdie!

DRACULA
Sits down

Thank you.

FUNNY SHORTS 2

VICKY

Wow, you're wearing a cape! I've never been out with a guy who wears a cape!

DRACULA

I always wear a cape. I would feel naked without it.

VICKY

It's such a classy touch! Most guys I meet can barely manage to shave before a date, so you got on my good side already, fella! Say, that's an interesting accent you got there. Where did you say you're from?

DRACULA

I am from an ancient country known as Transylvania.

VICKY

Hand in front of her mouth, whispering

Right. Geography was never my best subject, so just between you and me, Vlad, where exactly is Transylvania? Is it anywhere near Pennsylvania? It sounds like the name of a new identity category, or something! Does the "T" in LGBTQ stand for that? You're not a gender fluid type, are you? I mean, I'm a very tolerant gal, but I just don't know what to think about all these categories today. Things are getting so confusing, you don't know who you're talking to anymore!

DRACULA
Transylvania is my homeland. It is a very old country in the Carpathian Mountains.

VICKY
Mountains, ugh, I hate them. Well, I don't exactly "hate" them — I try not to hate anything. My spiritual adviser says hate is not good for your mental health. I'm just not an outdoorsy type, is all I'm saying. I think humans evolved to get away from the outdoors, don't you? I mean, outdoors you have bugs, bats, all sorts of icky things. Plus, I don't like going anyplace where I can't get my pumpkin spice lattes. I'm so addicted to them! Do they have Starbucks in Transylvania?

WAITRESS
Enters

Hi kids, my name is Diane and I'll be your waitress. How about I get youse something to drink?

FUNNY SHORTS 2

VICKY
I'll just take a water.

DRACULA
I will have a Bloody Mary, if you please.

WAITRESS
Sorry, we don't serve alcohol.

DRACULA
Then I will take a Virgin Mary.

WAITRESS
Look hon, we're short-staffed today, so if you don't mind, it's better to stick with the easy stuff, all right?

DRACULA
Then I require nothing.

WAITRESS
How about a water? We have sparkling or tap.

DRACULA
Grimaces

No water!

WAITRESS

Okay, got it, no water. Our specials today are honey-baked salmon with asparagus and grilled New York strip in a bourbon glaze. I'll give youse guys a second to decide.

She leaves

VICKY

I've heard the steak is very good here. I know we're all so health conscious these days, but sometimes I just like a nice juicy steak. You're not a vegan, are you?

DRACULA

I am not a vegan.

VICKY

That's a relief! I'm not opposed to veganism or anything, it's just that my relationship to food is so complicated these days. If you knew the way I used to eat! Omigod, I didn't care what I put in my mouth! I used to put peanut butter on potato chips, can you believe it? And I put ketchup on everything! I mean, if you'd have seen me eating a hamburger, I had so much ketchup on that sucker it looked like I had blood dripping from my mouth every time I took a bite. Can you picture that?

DRACULA

Yes. . . as a matter of fact, I can. So, Victoria, tell me about yourself. You are such an attractive young woman, with such a beautiful... neck. I would like to know more about you.

VICKY

Giggles, touching her neck

Well, thank you for the compliment! I have always felt that my neck is one of my assets. You're probably thinking, with a neck like that, why isn't she married? Well, it's a long, sad story, I'm afraid. My first trip down the aisle, I married my high school sweetheart. Boy that went south fast! He was so immature -- he never spent any time at home. He was always saying he needed to hang with his buddies! Why are guys like that, so attached to their buddies?

DRACULA

I would not know. I do not have *(pause)* buddies.

VICKY

Good for you! So, anyway, that marriage was doomed from the start. I was heartbroken when we split, but I just made the best of it. Went back to school, got my degree in phlebotomy, and now I have a good career taking blood samples at a lab. I've won the Employee Of The Month award ten times! You wouldn't believe how efficient I am at taking blood. I just feel it's better for the patients if I do it quickly. People can be very squeamish about getting their blood taken, you know.

DRACULA
Yes. As a matter of fact, I do know. Tell me, Victoria, do you have a key to the vault?

VICKY
Sorry, we don't have anybody named Walt in our office. There's a cute guy named Walt who works in the pizza shop next door, but--

DRACULA
No, no, I mean the place where they store the blood! The blood, Victoria!

WAITRESS
Enters, and Dracula is annoyed at the interruption

Okay, so are you kids ready to order?

FUNNY SHORTS 2

VICKY
Sure, I'll take the chicken Caesar salad, but put a little extra chicken on there, honey, will you? I need my protein today.

WAITRESS
No problem. Is there anything I can get you, big guy? We have a delicious salad today with fresh fruit — strawberries, blueberries, some blood oranges—

DRACULA
Pounds table

Why do you call them blood oranges? An orange has no blood!

Awkward silence

WAITRESS
Okay, no need to get your panties in a twist! I take it that means no salad for you.

DRACULA
I detest salad!

WAITRESS
Got it. I'll be back with your order, honey.
She leaves

DRACULA

So, let us get back to you, Victoria. Please tell me about your career drawing blood. I am very interested to know more about that. I imagine it is a very exciting job, is it not?

VICKY

My job is okay, but that's not the real Vicky. That's just what I do for a living. My love life is really much more interesting! So, getting back to that: it took awhile after my divorce, but slowly I started to date again. When your heart's broken, it's hard to put the pieces back together. I mean, you break up with someone, it's like having a stake driven through your heart, am I right?

DRACULA

Eyes widen, puts his hand on his chest

Did you say a stake? Through the heart?

VICKY

So, time goes by and then I meet this guy Tommy. He tells me he loves me, and it seems like he means it. He listens to me, we take long walks where we talk about all sorts of things, oh, everything looks wonderful. I'm thinking, I met my soul mate, the man of my dreams. I don't know if you've ever met anyone special like that.

DRACULA
Looks off into the distance

Once, many centuries ago, I had a forbidden love. It was a doomed love affair from the start. We were two souls joined together for the ages, with a love that could not speak its name. We were like--

VICKY

So anyway, Tommy and I get married. It goes well at first, but then slowly there are problems. The first thing is, he starts shutting me out. I mean, he's always glued to his computer or his phone or the TV, never seems to be paying attention when I'm talking to him. Then his company sends him on a three-week assignment to Patagonia to work on a computer system for a client, and he comes back and tells me he fell in love with a chambermaid in his hotel, some Patagonian girl who doesn't speak a word of English! Can you imagine? He leaves the next day and moves to Patagonia, and the last I heard he married this woman! I have no idea how she even communicates with him, because he doesn't speak any Patagonian. Can you imagine? Oh, good, here are our meals. I'm starving!

WAITRESS
Enters

Here youse go. Is there anything else youse guys need?

VICKY
No, this looks delicious.

DRACULA
I require nothing!

Waitress leaves

DRACULA
Now, Victoria, let us talk again about the laboratory where you work. I have always been interested in blood -- in a very scientific way of course. Would you please tell me if anyone works in the laboratory at night?

VICKY
Not listening

So after Tommy I married an older guy. I

thought it was going to last, but that one ended when he went crazy and burned all his hearing aids. I've been single ever since. I finally thought I'd try the online dating scene, and I've met my share of creepy characters, let me tell you. You don't seem creepy, though. I have to admit that it did bother me a little that you don't have a social media presence, but then again some people just like their privacy, right? I bet you're one of those people -- I get it, totally. I mean, the world today, everybody knows all your secrets, right?

DRACULA
I have many secrets. Many dark and mysterious secrets. But let us not talk about me, Victoria. Let us talk about you, and your career of drawing blood --

VICKY
And then there's the constant chatter! It's just never-ending, isn't it? All the pressure to be part of that online conversation, that goes on and on and on, it just literally never stops, does it? People yakking and yakking about their boring lives! But, really, I should stop talking about me, me, me, and ask you a few questions about yourself. So tell me, are you religious? I mean, you're wearing black –

omigod, you didn't take a vow of celibacy or anything crazy like that, did you?

DRACULA
Religion, bah! I have an ancient quarrel with God, and that is why I am cursed, condemned to roam the world, banished from society, a solitary being who haunts the lonely hours of the night, a lost soul, a—

VICKY
I'm not religious myself. All that stuff about thou shalt and thou shalt not, it's just too controlling, don't you think? I think that's going too far, even for a Supreme Being. So let's move on to your career, shall we? That's very important, in my book. I'll be blunt here, Vlad: I don't like men who don't do an honest day's work. You know the type — out all night, sleep all day. You're not one of those types, are you?

DRACULA
Stares at her, holds out his hands with fingers outstretched as if trying to hypnotize her

Look into my eyes, Victoria. Look deep into my eyes. You are now completely in my power. You can think only of doing my will. You wish to fly away with me, to become my slave forever. You are totally under my control, Victoria. You will do exactly what I say.

VICKY
Stares at him for a moment, then goes back to talking

Do you like to travel? I have to admit I get a little nervous on airplanes, although it's nothing that a glass or three of wine won't solve, LOL! Sometimes when the ride gets a little bumpy, I've been known to grab for the person sitting next to me. I get so flustered I don't know what I'm grabbing — the last time it happened I was sitting next to a priest, and well, THAT was a bit uncomfortable. Boy, I never knew priests used that kind of language!

DRACULA
Shaken, talking to himself, looking at his hands

I do not understand. My power has always been absolute. No one can resist when I gaze into their eyes. What is this strange power she has?

FUNNY SHORTS 2

VICKY

You know, in spite of all the things that have happened to me in my romantic life, I'm still a person who likes to look on the sunny side of life. That's just me, what can I say? You can always find the sunshine in life, don't you agree?

DRACULA

Groans

I hate sunshine!

VICKY

Now, look, Vlad, this is only the first time we're meeting, so let's talk a few ground rules about the whole sex thing, okay? Foreplay is very important to me, maybe a little nibbling on my ear—okay, I admit there have been times when in the heat of passion there's been a little more — maybe a teeny tiny love bite or two. I can get a little out of control, to be honest with you!

DRACULA

Puts his hand on his neck

Did you say love bite?

VICKY

Yes, but like I said, we'd have to know each other a lot better before that happens. I mean, hundreds and hundreds, maybe thousands of conversations! We'd be sharing really intimate things like our favorite flavor of ice cream, what TV shows make us cry, that type of sharing. I'm sure you'll agree that we need to get to know each other better, right? I'm just not interested in short-term relationships, I want to find a man I can fall in love with for all eternity.

DRACULA

Eternity? With you, Victoria?

VICKY

Yes, that's exactly what I'm saying! Wouldn't it be so romantic? Sharing all my deepest, most intimate thoughts about everything with you. A conversation that would go on and on and on for eternity. Wouldn't that be the best?

DRACULA
Suddenly stands up

I must leave – immediately!

VICKY

What? So fast?

FUNNY SHORTS 2

DRACULA
I have an appointment and I must leave – now! *(bows)* It was *(pause)* quite educational to meet you. Goodbye.

Turns to go, then turns back suddenly

Do not communicate with me again, Victoria!

VICKY
Oh, okay, goodbye.

Dracula exits, waitress enters

WAITRESS
What, your friend left?

VICKY
Yes. I just don't know what it is with guys these days -- you'd think they're afraid I'm going to bite them!

THE END

FUNNY SHORTS 2

GRILLING WHITEY

CHARACTERS

DETECTIVE JOE RADISH — A Detective in the Nutrition Division of the police force. He is around 40, trim, athletic, wearing a short sleeved shirt and tie. His suit jacket is on the back of the chair in front of him.

WHITEY — A career bad eater. He is in his 30s. He also wears a suit, but his tie is askew and his clothes are rumpled. He is nervous, but tries to hide it with a show of bravado.

SETTING

Note: the actors speak like characters in a 1940s gangster movie.

An interrogation room at the police station. Whitey is sitting at a table. There is another chair, and Detective Radish is standing with his knee bent and one foot on it. He peers intently at Whitey. Sometimes he takes his foot off the chair and moves around the room. Other times he leans close to Whitey, to intimidate him.

TIME

Present.

DETECTIVE RADISH
Hello Whitey. The name's Radish. Detective Joe Radish.

WHITEY
Yeah, yeah. Listen, copper, when are you mugs going to let me out of here?

DETECTIVE RADISH
Never mind that. It's time to talk turkey. Free range turkey.

WHITEY
You'll get nothin' out of me, copper.

DETECTIVE RADISH
Think you're a tough guy, huh? I've seen your type before. You'll fold like a cheap suit.

WHITEY
In your dreams, copper.

DETECTIVE RADISH
Yeah? We'll see about that. Where were you the night before last?

FUNNY SHORTS 2

WHITEY
I was home, making a salad. With lettuce, tomatoes – all organic, of course. Oh, and extra virgin olive oil – I'm very picky about my olive oil, see?

DETECTIVE RADISH
You got any witnesses?

WHITEY
No. Nobody was home but me. I don't like anyone around when I make salad.

DETECTIVE RADISH
Ha! A likely story.

WHITEY
It's the truth, Radish.

DETECTIVE RADISH
That's Detective Radish to you. And you're lying, Whitey.

WHITEY
Yeah, says who?

DETECTIVE RADISH
Says me. I think you were doing something else, not making salad.

FUNNY SHORTS 2

WHITEY
Like what, copper?

DETECTIVE RADISH
Like eating fries, Whitey. French fries.

WHITEY
Hah! You can't pin that on me. I've been on the Paleo diet for years. I ain't one of them processed food palookas.

DETECTIVE RADISH
You think you're a smart cookie, don't you? You think you can put one over on the law, don't you?

WHITEY
I'm smarter than you, if that's what you mean.

DETECTIVE RADISH
You think so? Well, I just might have something up my sleeve.

WHITEY
You ain't got nothin' up your sleeve, copper. You're wearin' a short sleeve shirt.

DETECTIVE RADISH
Oh, a comedian, huh? Think you're funny, huh?

FUNNY SHORTS 2

WHITEY
I like a few laughs now and then.

DETECTIVE RADISH
Well, see if you get a laugh out of this *(holds up an empty fast food carton of French fries)* Look familiar, Whitey?

WHITEY
I never laid eyes on that in my life. I don't even know what it is.

DETECTIVE RADISH
waves it underneath his nose

Let me help you out. Recognize that smell? Little strips of potatoes deep fried in polyunsaturated fats? It's the smell of crime, Whitey.

WHITEY
You got nothin', copper. It won't hold up in court. You got no proof, see?

DETECTIVE RADISH
The game's up, Whitey. You got ratted out.

WHITEY
Yeah, by who?

DETECTIVE RADISH
Your neighbor, the cute little number from apartment 12B – Janice Kale.

WHITEY
Janice Kale?

DETECTIVE RADISH
That's right, Janice Kale. She ratted on you, Whitey. Gave us the goods on you — she swiped this *(holds up French fry container again)* from your kitchen trash can when you weren't looking.

WHITEY
You're lyin'! Janice would never do that.

DETECTIVE RADISH
It's the truth, Whitey. And you want to know why she did it?

WHITEY
Why, copper?

DETECTIVE RADISH
You're playing dirty at the dinner table, Whitey, and Janice can't stomach it no more.

FUNNY SHORTS 2

WHITEY

Janice would never rat me out! We're in love. We go out to the pictures together. Sometimes we stay home and watch them shows on TV about how to make healthy meals. Nah, Janice would never do that. We're in love, I tell ya!

DETECTIVE RADISH

Love don't trump good nutrition, kid.

WHITEY

You're all wrong, copper! Janice and me, we got somethin' special. We got a love that lasts. We're soul mates, you get me?

DETECTIVE RADISH

Sorry, Whitey. Janice wised up to your act. She knows all your dirty secrets – the milkshakes you drink on the sly, the candy bars you hide under the couch, the cute little cupcakes you take to bed with you. It's a dark story, Whitey, and Janice finally saw the light.

WHITEY

Janice? My true love? Oh, it's a dirty, rotten world! I thought I had one bright spot in this crummy world, one place where I had something special, one person who wouldn't care about my dietary habits!

FUNNY SHORTS 2

DETECTIVE RADISH

Janice is a stand up girl, Whitey. She did the right thing. People start eating French fries, drinking soda pop, the next thing you know the world don't make sense anymore. It just goes all screwy, you get me?

WHITEY

I thought I had her fooled. I just couldn't give up my burgers and fries, my macaroni and cheese, my Tutti Frutti ice cream – I tried, but I couldn't do it! We used to snuggle up on the couch to watch TV, and she'd feed me cauliflower – you ever eat raw cauliflower, copper? It oughta be against the law! I couldn't take it after a while -- I'd try to play along, just to make her happy, but inside I was dyin' for somethin' bad for me -- a box of jelly doughnuts, a stack of pancakes drippin' with maple syrup, or somethin' really bad, like a double hot fudge sundae with M&Ms on it. You understand, don't you, copper?

DETECTIVE RADISH

I'll never understand guys like you, Whitey. You got a healthy little number like Janice Kale waitin' at home for you, but instead you gotta go for the candy, the fried food, the saturated fats. No, Janice Kale is the smart one, kid. She knows what counts in this world. Do you know what counts, Whitey?

WHITEY

What?

DETECTIVE RADISH

Calories — that's what counts. She came to us because your calorie count was too high.

WHITEY

Who woulda thought my sweet Janice would stab me in the gut like this?

DETECTIVE RADISH

You're going to the chair, Whitey. You're going to fry for this.

WHITEY

You can't fry me! Not that! Please, copper! I promise, I'll never do it again! Can't you put in a word for me with the judge?

DETECTIVE RADISH

I can't make deals like that, Whitey. The Feds have nutritional guidelines, you know that, you sap. You don't follow the guidelines, you gotta pay the price. My hands are tied.

WHITEY

Just one more chance — please, copper! You gotta understand, I had a disadvantaged childhood, see? I never knew my Dad — he was a chemist who made dirty deals with the junk food boys and ended up face down in a landfill. And my ma, all she cared about was her next Big Mac. I wanted love, but all she gave me was clogged arteries. How could you expect me to turn out different, with folks like that?

DETECTIVE RADISH

Don't blame it on your parents, Whitey. They may have been bad eggs, but you had choices. You just made the wrong ones, kid, that's all.

WHITEY

I can't fry! I can't! There must be somethin' you can do, copper.

DETECTIVE RADISH

Well, maybe there is one thing, Whitey.

WHITEY

Anything! I'll do anything!

DETECTIVE RADISH

I can't make any promises, you understand.

It's just, I may be able to put in a word for you, get your sentence reduced to life without parole at a free range chicken farm. You'll have to clean a lot of chicken coops, kid, but at least you won't fry. No guarantees, though!

WHITEY
That's aces with me! Whatever you can do!

DETECTIVE RADISH
I'll need something from you, kid.

WHITEY
You got it, copper!

DETECTIVE RADISH
I need the names of the people in your apartment building who aren't eating healthy.

WHITEY
No! It's too much — you're askin' me to rat out my neighbors. I can't do that, Radish!

DETECTIVE RADISH
It figures. I knew you'd be too yellow to do the right thing, Whitey. Okay, suit yourself. I'll be leaving now. *(starts to go)*

WHITEY
Wait! *(pause)*. I'm gonna hate myself for this, but okay. You got me over a barrel, copper, so I'll do it.

DETECTIVE RADISH
Good, I knew you'd come around.

WHITEY
It's a dirty job you're askin' me to do, and it won't be easy.

DETECTIVE RADISH
Aw, it's a piece of cake, Whitey — sugar free cake, of course. All you got to do is hang around on trash night, look inside a few garbage cans. It's simple — you just keep your eyes and ears open, read some labels, swipe some junk food wrappers, some empty soda pop bottles, and you'll get all the information we need.

WHITEY
You want me to trash dive? Is that what you're sayin'?

DETECTIVE RADISH
That's what I'm sayin'.

FUNNY SHORTS 2

WHITEY

I could get killed! People don't take kindly to mugs like me lookin' in their trash cans, copper.

DETECTIVE RADISH

Well, you don't play nice with me, you're gonna fry anyway, Whitey. At least this way, you got a chance. Just stay on your toes, kid, and you'll be fine.

WHITEY

Thinks it over

All right, I'll do it. I don't like it, but I'll do it.

DETECTIVE RADISH

That's the spirit, Whitey. I'll get the judge to let you out on bail, and you'll be back at your place in time for trash night. I'll give you a bullet-proof vest to wear, just in case your trigger happy neighbors get any ideas about making you into a piece of Swiss cheese.

WHITEY

Thanks, that's big of you.

DETECTIVE RADISH

This'll help us, Whitey. We've got our eye on a

couple of mugs in your building, and this will give us the goods on them.

WHITEY

Whatever you say, copper. It looks like I ain't got much choice at this point.

DETECTIVE RADISH

That's right, Whitey. But I'm hoping you'll go straight now, kid. You don't want to be a junk food addict all your life, do you? It's time to break that sugar habit, get off the polyunsaturated fat train, stop feeding that sweet tooth. You'll feel better about yourself, see? And maybe that cute little Janice Kale will give you a second chance. You'd like that, wouldn't you?

WHITEY

Yeah, I'd like that. Janice Kale was the best thing that ever happened to me. I can't believe I sacrificed a tomato like her for a couple of lousy cheeseburgers. You know, copper, maybe it's time for me to start down a new road, become a new man, turn my life around.

DETECTIVE RADISH

Sounds like a good decision, Whitey. You won't regret it.

FUNNY SHORTS 2

WHITEY
Thanks. Hey, I could use a cup of joe. You got any?

DETECTIVE RADISH
Yeah, sure. Here you go.

Pours a cup of coffee and hands it to Whitey.

WHITEY
Thanks.

Takes a drink, spits it out.

DETECTIVE RADISH
Hey, what did you do that for?

WHITEY
Black coffee? I never drink it black! Ain't you got any sugar in this joint?

DETECTIVE RADISH
You stupid mug, when will you get it through your thick head? Sugar kills!

WHITEY
Sorry, copper, I won't do it again.

FUNNY SHORTS 2

DETECTIVE RADISH

All right, Whitey. I just hope you finally get it. You can't be a good citizen when you're eatin' bad.

Puts his hand on Whitey's shoulder.

Okay, kid, it's back to the slammer for now.

WHITEY

I can't take much more of that food they serve in this joint. Nothin' but bread and water – it ain't enough for a guy like me, Radish!

DETECTIVE RADISH

I'll see if I can get them to slip you a cookie now and then, Whitey. It's the least I can do, since you're cooperatin'.

WHITEY

Thanks, Radish. You're an okay guy.

DETECTIVE RADISH

Just doin' my job, kid. All right, let's go.

Whitey gets up, and they leave.

THE END

LOVE YOU MADLY

CHARACTERS

JAYNE   Twentyish. A bit bookish-looking, and in fact is reading a book as the play starts.

DOUGLAS   Same age as Jayne, but with a more extroverted manner. He is dramatic in his gestures.

NATASHA   Also same age. Is dressed more stylishly, and has a somewhat domineering manner.

SETTING

A Food Court at a mall. Jayne is sitting at a table reading a book. There is a small trashcan next to her. Douglas enters and sits down at the table. Natasha is offstage at first.

TIME

Evening.

NOTE: Jayne and Douglas must alternate between their normal mannerisms and voices, and exaggerated, overly dramatic gestures and voices when they are "acting" for Natasha's benefit.

DOUGLAS
Enters in a hurry

Excuse me, could I sit here? Just for a moment. I'm sorry, but it's really, really important.

JAYNE
But there are other open tables--

DOUGLAS
Sits down

Thank you! I really appreciate this. Also, could we talk?

JAYNE
Talk?

DOUGLAS
Yes, talk. Have a conversation. Or pretend to. I need to look like I'm talking to you.

JAYNE
But why?

DOUGLAS
It's really complicated, but there's a person over there I don't want to talk to. If I'm talking to you, she won't come over.

JAYNE
Look, I don't want to get involved in your personal—

DOUGLAS
I know it's a lot to ask, but this is a dicey situation, and I need some help.

JAYNE
Are you in danger? What's this about?

DOUGLAS
I'm not at liberty to say, but trust me, it's not dangerous. Please, I really need this. You'd be doing an act of charity.

JAYNE
I don't know...

DOUGLAS
Look, we're in the Food Court at the mall. It's totally safe here. I just need you to pretend you're having a conversation with me for a few minutes. I swear, just for a few minutes, and that's it. It's perfectly safe, trust me. Although it has to be convincing, or things could get ugly fast.

JAYNE
I thought you said this wasn't dangerous!

DOUGLAS
Well, not for you. You're perfectly fine. Look, just pretend we know each other, okay? It's acting, that's all. I'm sure you can act. I bet you were in your high school shows, right?

JAYNE
No I wasn't.

DOUGLAS
Never mind, just play along till she goes away.

JAYNE
Okay, I guess I could play along a little.

DOUGLAS
So, how's your love life?

JAYNE

Hey, what is this? Are you trying to hit on me?

DOUGLAS

Whispers

I'm pretending, remember? Just making it up.

JAYNE

Oh, right. But can we just talk about the weather or something?

DOUGLAS

Okay, fine. It's a beautiful day, isn't it?

JAYNE

Self-consciously acting

Yes it is quite beautiful.

DOUGLAS

It's a gorgeous day to hang out with a gorgeous person, wouldn't you say?

JAYNE

Stops acting for a moment

What? I don't think this conversation is--

DOUGLAS

Whispers

Come on, just play along.

JAYNE
Acting again

Okay. Yes it is.

DOUGLAS

You're the kind of woman a man could really fall in love with. I'll bet you have a special someone in your life, right? *(He urges her on, nodding his head).*

JAYNE
Still acting

Actually, not at the moment.

DOUGLAS

Really? I'm shocked. I mean, I would give anything to go out with you. If I was your boyfriend, I'd treat you like a princess.

JAYNE
She looks shocked

DOUGLAS
Whispers

Just pretending, remember?

JAYNE

Oh, right. *(Acting)* Thank you, but I'm not interested in relationships right now.

DOUGLAS

Oh, that's too bad. Is it because you were hurt?

JAYNE

Dramatically

Yes. My last relationship left me shattered. Broken. A shell of myself.

DOUGLAS

That's terrible!

JAYNE

I thought he was the one for me. That's what makes it so hard.

DOUGLAS

I know what you mean. I'm on the rebound too. I had someone I really thought was my soulmate, but it didn't work out.

JAYNE

I'm sorry.

DOUGLAS
I didn't know if I'd ever recover. There was a big hole in my life after she left.

JAYNE
I know how that feels. It's so terrible.

DOUGLAS
I was a pitiful, broken man, who didn't think he'd ever love again. *(Beat)* Until I met you.

JAYNE
Really committing to the game

I feel the same way!

DOUGLAS
Isn't it wonderful that we met?

JAYNE
It really is.

DOUGLAS
I'm so glad I found you *(holds her hand).* I'm deeply, madly in love with you!

JAYNE
Stops acting, takes her hand back

Uh, wait a minute.

DOUGLAS
Grabs her hand again

You have such sensitivity, such a big heart. You're a romantic like me, I can tell. You like puppy dogs and flowers and soft ballads. We're meant for each other.

JAYNE
Takes her hand back

I'm more of a cat person, actually.

DOUGLAS
Grabs her hand again

You're it — you're the one for me.

JAYNE

No, no, no *(takes her hand back)*. I think we should just stop now.

DOUGLAS

Why? I'm listening to my heart, and my heart is telling me you're the one.

JAYNE
Starts to move her chair back

I have to go now.

DOUGLAS
Whispers

Just playing a game, remember? It's not for real.

JAYNE
Whispers

Are you sure?

DOUGLAS
I'm not interested in you at all. Not even a little bit. Not if you were the last woman on Earth. Not if I was on a desert island and you were—

JAYNE
Okay, I get it.

DOUGLAS
I just don't want HER to notice I'm alone.

JAYNE
Are you trying to make her jealous?

DOUGLAS
Her? I have no feelings for her! She's nothing to me. She's dead, dead to me, that's what she is!

FUNNY SHORTS 2

JAYNE
Looks offstage

Well, good, because she's coming over here.

NATASHA
Enters

Hello, Douglas.

DOUGLAS
Hello Natasha.

NATASHA
Fancy running in to you here.

DOUGLAS
Yes, well, it's just one of those things, I guess.

NATASHA
Who is this, your new girlfriend?

JAYNE
No, actually, I'm just—

DOUGLAS
Yes she is, Natasha. She's nicer to me than you. She's got a heart. She's not a cold, unfeeling bitch like you. She's a real person!

NATASHA
Hello, it's nice to meet you, Real Person. What's your name?

DOUGLAS
Her name is Honey, not that you would care.

NATASHA
Honey? That's the name you gave me, Douglas! How could you take the pet name you gave me and use it for this shameless hussy who—

DOUGLAS
It fits her better, Natasha. She really is as sweet as honey, unlike you.

NATASHA
You jerk!

JAYNE
It's not really my name. Jayne is my name. It's spelled with a Y, like J-A-Y-N-E? I know it's not the usual spelling, but--

NATASHA
I'm done with you, Douglas. I'm through! You'll never hurt me again!

DOUGLAS
I'm done with you too, Natasha! I never want to see you ever again!

NATASHA
Well you won't, you jerk, because I'm going to blow your brains out right here.

JAYNE
Excuse me, what's going on here?

DOUGLAS
You wouldn't do it, Natasha. Want to know why? You haven't got the guts.

NATASHA
Oh yeah? Well I'll show you!

Natasha reaches in her handbag and points it at him as if there's a gun inside.

JAYNE
I'm sure that's not necessary! Not necessary at all! I was just sitting here, reading my book, and Douglas sat down and—

NATASHA
This is the end, Douglas, for you and your girlfriend!

JAYNE
But I'm not his girlfriend. Not at all. For one thing, he likes dogs, and I'm a cat person, and—

DOUGLAS
Go ahead, do it, Natasha! And while you're at it, why don't you shoot Honey here too? I mean, it's really her fault — she seduced me.

NATASHA
What are you talking about?

DOUGLAS
I'm the victim here, you know. Her flirty manner and her voluptuous body, that's what turned my head. I lost it, Natasha, I just couldn't help myself.

NATASHA
Well, you always did like the slutty looking ones, Douglas.

JAYNE
Slutty? I don't believe this!

DOUGLAS
Don't listen to a word she says, Natasha. She's

a lying viper who collects men like trophies. She destroys their lives, breaks their hearts, and then throws them away like broken toys. She's evil!

JAYNE
Are you kidding me? You're the one who sat down here and—

NATASHA
Looking at Jayne

I have to admit, she looks the type, Douglas.

JAYNE
I am not a viper! If anything, I'm the victim here!

DOUGLAS
Look at her, lying like that! She's so natural at it!

NATASHA
To Jayne

You really have no shame, do you?

DOUGLAS
I'm sorry, Natasha. I shouldn't have done it.

NATASHA
It's okay, Douglas. You just couldn't help it — I can see that now.

JAYNE
I wouldn't touch him with a ten-foot pole! If you think that for one moment—

DOUGLAS
Will you ever forgive me, Natasha?

NATASHA
Of course, my darling. Come with me, and we'll get a few shots at our favorite espresso bar. Then we'll go back to my place for some randy fun. Remember all the fun we used to have?

DOUGLAS
Do I! Natasha, you've just made me a very happy man.

NATASHA
Together again, just like the old times, Douglas!

JAYNE
I can't believe this!

NATASHA
To Jayne

Goodbye, "Honey", or whatever your real name is. And just remember, you can't treat men like playthings. They have feelings, and they'll always come back to the woman who really loves them. Douglas, let's go, darling.

DOUGLAS
Gets up

I feel sorry for her, dear.

NATASHA

Yes, it's a pity. But people like her will get their just desserts. She'll probably die alone and unloved, as punishment for all her evil deeds. Well, let's be off, my love.

DOUGLAS

Yes, you sweet thing, let's go!

They leave

JAYNE
Looks at her book

"How To Live A More Exciting Life." *She throws the book into the trashcan next to her.* No thank you!

THE END

FUNNY SHORTS 2

CANDY HEART

FUNNY SHORTS 2

CHARACTERS

BILLY WILSON	A motivational speaker, fiftyish. He talks in slogans and is very emotional. Has a hidden sweet tooth.
MRS. BENSON	The longtime owner of a candy store. Grandmotherly, but tough. Seventyish.

SETTING

The candy store.

TIME

Late afternoon.

At rise, Mrs. Benson is standing behind the candy counter. Billy enters.

BILLY WILSON

Hello Mrs. Benson! Do you remember me? Billy Wilson? I used to come in here all the time as a kid.

MRS. BENSON

Sorry young man, I don't recognize you.

BILLY WILSON

Totally understandable, no problem. It's been a long time, and, besides, I'm a completely different person now. It's like night and day, how different I am from that little boy who used to come in here!

MRS. BENSON

That's nice. Would you like to buy some candy?

BILLY WILSON

Want to know why I'm in town? I'm doing a book signing at the mall over in Parkersburg.

FUNNY SHORTS 2

MRS. BENSON
A book signing? Who did you say you were?

BILLY WILSON
Strikes a pose. He has one hand on his hip, and with the other hand he is pointing his finger at Mrs. Benson.

Recognize this pose?

MRS. BENSON
Taken aback

Uh, no.

BILLY WILSON
Or, how about this catchphrase: "Screw the past!" From TV? You've seen my TV specials? My videos? My late night infomercials?

MRS. BENSON
Sorry, I'm not much of a TV person. What does "Screw the past" mean?

BILLY WILSON
It means throwing off the baggage of your old life! I help people throw away their old life just like you throw away a used candy wrapper! I show them how to get rid of the past and

become a totally different person! I don't take any alibis though — I'm hard on them, and I won't let people give me excuses for why they're not achieving more. And you know what's the best part?

MRS. BENSON
What?

BILLY WILSON
I'm living proof that it can be done, that with discipline and hard work you can transform yourself into the person you've always wanted to be!

MRS. BENSON
That's wonderful, young man. So, would you like some candy?

BILLY WILSON
Ah, look at that. The candy counter! I remember that so well. You used to sell the best penny candy.

MRS. BENSON
I have them all — red hot dollars, gumdrops, licorice, malted milk balls, candy cigarettes, lollipops — the kids all love this place.

BILLY WILSON
You had those little brown paper bags, and you'd fill them with one of this, two of that — whatever I wanted. It was so much fun to pick out the candy! This is really bringing me back. I don't usually have time for nostalgia in my life, but just this once I'll allow myself to indulge.

MRS. BENSON
You say you came in here a lot?

BILLY WILSON
All the time. I practically lived in this store.

MRS. BENSON
I wish I could remember you, I really do. What did you say your name was?

BILLY WILSON
Billy Wilson. Actually, more people knew me by my nickname.

MRS. BENSON
Oh? What was it?

BILLY WILSON
It was a long time ago, ha ha. *(Beat)*

MRS. BENSON
Yes?

BILLY WILSON
A really long time ago! Years and years ago – another lifetime!

MRS. BENSON
That's nice. But what was your nickname?

BILLY WILSON
Clears his throat

Chubby.

MRS. BENSON
Oh my goodness, you're Chubby Wilson?

BILLY WILSON
In the flesh. Of course, that was SO many years ago, and—

MRS. BENSON
You lost all your fat!

BILLY WILSON
That's right, I lost all of it — you see, I had my breakthrough moment and—

FUNNY SHORTS 2

MRS. BENSON
You were a real roly-poly little boy, weren't you?

BILLY WILSON
Yes, back in the old days I was. But now—

MRS. BENSON
I remember how your clothes never fit you — your pants were always so tight, and your stomach hung so far over your belt buckle.

BILLY WILSON
I don't really remember.

MRS. BENSON
Of all the children I served here over the years, I think you were the fattest.

BILLY WILSON
Oh? Heh, heh, that's quite a distinction, I guess.

MRS. BENSON
My, you were quite a size! I used to wonder how you were able to tie your shoelaces. It must have been nearly impossible! I bet you had to get someone else to do it for you, right?

FUNNY SHORTS 2

BILLY WILSON
I don't...I don't remember. It's been so long ago, and I'm really so much different now. I'm sure you can tell how much I've changed, and--

MRS. BENSON
Chubby Wilson! Imagine you coming back in the store! Why, I'm amazed you didn't die of diabetes or heart disease, or one of those other things that fat people die of.

BILLY WILSON
Yes. *(grits his teeth)* I'll tell you the truth, Mrs. Benson. I didn't just come in here on a whim. I actually had a purpose in walking through that door. When I saw I'd be doing that book signing in Parkersburg, I decided to make a special trip here to celebrate just how far I've come in my life.

MRS. BENSON
Is that so?

BILLY WILSON
And you know what I learned, Mrs. Benson?

MRS. BENSON
What?

BILLY WILSON
That closure takes guts! Come to think of it, that's a great title for my next book — "Closure Takes Guts!" I like the way that sounds.

MRS. BENSON
Closure? What's that?

BILLY WILSON
Putting an end to the trauma of my childhood. Truth be told, it was a trauma you caused, Mrs. Benson.

MRS. BENSON
Me?

BILLY WILSON
Yes you, Mrs. Benson, I don't know if you recall this, but you were the person who gave me that horrible nickname. It was you who started calling me Chubby every time I came in here. It was you who used to give me extra candy because you said I had a bigger appetite. It was you who told me not to sit down or I'd break one of your chairs. Do you remember that, Mrs. Benson?

MRS. BENSON
No, can't say I do, young man.

FUNNY SHORTS 2

BILLY WILSON
Well, you did it! And it damaged me, Mrs. Benson!

MRS. BENSON
I joked around a lot with the kids. It was all in fun.

BILLY WILSON
Heh, heh, I doubt that nine-year-old Billy Wilson would use the word "fun" to describe it. But no matter, I'm over it now. It's all in the past. *(Turns toward the door)*. In fact, I'm so over it that I'm just going to walk out that door now and say a final goodbye to my past. Goodbye, Mrs. Benson!

MRS. BENSON
I don't think a little kidding around ever hurt anyone.

BILLY WILSON
Getting angry

Kidding? It was more than kidding, Mrs. Benson. No, you had a special torture for little Billy Wilson, didn't you? Do you remember Valentine's Day when I was 12 and I came in here to buy a bag of those candy hearts for a girl in school — do you remember that?

MRS. BENSON
No, I can't say I do.

BILLY WILSON
I had such a crush on a girl in my class — Kelly Hobson, her name was. Oh, I was madly in love with her. I used to dream about her silky hair, her warm smile, her musical laugh. She was everything I ever wanted in a girl! I came here to buy some of those candy hearts for her, the ones with the little sayings on them, like, "Be Mine Forever," and when I told you who it was for, what did you do?

MRS. BENSON
What did I do?

BILLY WILSON
You laughed! It was a big, loud laugh that seemed to echo all down the block! And then, as if that wasn't enough, you told Kelly Hobson's mother the next time she came in the store that I was giving her daughter the candy hearts, and then you said — "that is, if he doesn't eat them all first".

MRS. BENSON
I said that?

BILLY WILSON
Yes, you did, Mrs. Benson! And she told Kelly, and Kelly told the whole class! It was cruel, Mrs. Benson. You're not really a sweet old lady, are you?

MRS. BENSON
Actually, I've always thought of myself as like those chocolate covered marshmallows over there — hard on the outside, but with a soft center.

BILLY WILSON
Wrong! You're more like a peanut chew — hard on the outside and hard on the inside! In fact, you're evil, sick, and twisted! You created trauma in an innocent boy, all because of your sick sense of humor! Don't you have a shred of remorse for what you did to me, Mrs. Benson?

MRS. BENSON
I think you're making a mountain out of a molehill, young man. Just because I made a few comments. I mean, you really were quite a size, you know.

BILLY WILSON
That's it, I've heard enough! A sadist like you doesn't deserve to live. I'm going to kill you,

before you ruin one more little boy's life the way you ruined mine!

Grabs a knife from the counter

Prepare to die, Mrs. Benson!

MRS. BENSON
But that's the knife I use to cut fudge.

BILLY WILSON
What more appropriate weapon? It has a special irony, doesn't it? The candy store owner gets killed with her fudge knife. *(insane laugh)* Ha, ha, ha! You know, I was testing you when I came in this shop, and you failed miserably. If you were kind to me when I came in the door I would have spared you, but you had to dwell on that horrible nickname, the name I haven't heard in so many years —

MRS. BENSON
What did you want me to call you — Skinny? It's a sin to lie, young man.

BILLY WILSON
You just don't get it, do you? I've had enough: say your prayers, you evil woman!

FUNNY SHORTS 2

MRS. BENSON
But people always give each other horrible nicknames. You wouldn't believe what I was called in high school.

BILLY WILSON
This is about my childhood, not yours! I'm here to avenge the trauma, and pay you back for all the pain you put me through. Prepare to die!

MRS. BENSON
Whatever you say, young man. But it does seem a shame to let all this candy go to waste.

BILLY WILSON
What do you mean, "go to waste"?

MRS. BENSON
If you kill me you'll have to run out of here fast before the police come, and then of course they'll throw all the candy away because nobody will want to eat candy from a store where the owner was murdered. All that sweet, lovely candy will go to waste.

BILLY WILSON
Why should I care about a few red hot dollars, a few malted milk balls, a few of those mouth-

watering chocolate coins wrapped in gold foil? Huh? Give me one good reason!

MRS. BENSON
It's just a shame, is all. Would you like to have some candy before you stab me?

BILLY WILSON
You can't be serious.

MRS. BENSON
Yes I am. I could make up a bag for you right now. Free of charge. I'll give you whatever you want.

BILLY WILSON
   Beat

Are those gumdrops over there?

MRS. BENSON
Yep. Just got a new order of them. There's nothing like gumdrops when they're fresh!

BILLY WILSON
I haven't had them in ages.

MRS. BENSON
They're still delicious. Want some?

FUNNY SHORTS 2

BILLY WILSON
Okay, just one or two, but then I'm going to slice you up like a pound of fudge, Mrs. Benson!

MRS. BENSON
Puts candy in a bag while she's talking

How about the licorice? I have it in six flavors. Want one of each?

BILLY WILSON
I don't care for the red kind.

MRS. BENSON
Oh, right, now I remember. That's about the only thing you didn't like in here, as I recall. Well, we'll just give you a couple of extra gumdrops. How about some chocolate drops? Some malted milk balls?

BILLY WILSON
Ah, they were the best, the malted milk balls. They just melted in your mouth.

MRS. BENSON
Filling the bag up

Right you are. Now, let's get you some more.

Why don't you just put that knife down while I keep filling this bag up. You might need two hands to carry this when I'm finished, Chubby!

BILLY WILSON

There you go again! I should have known not to trust you — people like you never change, do you? You're still a monster inside, a cruel, heartless monster! I'm going to do the one thing that will finally ease my pain — I'm going to—

He raises the knife

MRS. BENSON

Now, now, I'm just a prisoner of my upbringing. I grew up in a time when people thought it was important to tear each other down a little bit, otherwise you'd have a bunch of puffed up egomaniacs running the world, and where would we all be then? It was sort of a public service we were doing.

BILLY WILSON

A public service! To scar people for life?

MRS. BENSON

Oh, tosh. Look at you — why, you're as

successful as a man can be, from the looks of it. You just have that air about you of authority, success, money — all of it!

MRS. BENSON

BILLY WILSON

I do?

MRS. BENSON

Absolutely! You walked in here, and I said to myself, there's a man who's at the top of his field, a mover and shaker, a doer, somebody who's done really big things!

BILLY WILSON

Well, I've had a success or two, I admit.

MRS. BENSON

I can tell! Why, you're the picture of success! And you lost all that weight! I think you should be very proud of yourself, young man.

BILLY WILSON

You think so?

MRS. BENSON

I know so.

BILLY WILSON

It's funny, I do have some good memories of

this place. It still gives me a warm feeling, like when you're a kid and your stomach is full and the world seems safe.

MRS. BENSON
Well, that's what we're here for. Okay, there you go — a good selection of candy, free of charge. It'll take you all afternoon to finish that! You can go ahead and stab me now, Chubby.

Beat

BILLY WILSON
Look, I'm willing to forget all this if you'll do one thing for me.

MRS. BENSON
What's that?

BILLY WILSON
Stop calling me Chubby.

MRS. BENSON
What'd you say your name was?

BILLY WILSON
Billy. Billy Wilson.

MRS. BENSON
Well, Mr. Billy Wilson, it's nice to meet you! *(shakes his hand).* I think you're a shining example of what a man can do to change his life. I'm glad you stopped in today — it makes me feel good about humanity to see someone like you out there walking around.

BILLY WILSON
Thank you, that was nice to hear. *(Beat)* Um, I should go. I have to go to my—

MRS. BENSON
I know. Book signing.

BILLY WILSON
Yes, right. I'll just take my candy and leave.

MRS. BENSON
Certainly. But can I have my fudge knife back?

BILLY WILSON
Hands the knife to her

Yes, of course. Sorry about all the — um — shouting and everything.

MRS. BENSON
No problem at all. Stop back anytime.

BILLY WILSON
I'll think about it. If I get out this way again.

MRS. BENSON
Good boy. It's a scary world out there, and candy stores are a safe haven, don't you think? My motto is, "No day is complete without something sweet." Isn't that nice?

BILLY WILSON
Yes, it is. Goodbye, Mrs. Benson.

MRS. BENSON
Goodbye, young man.

Billy leaves.

MRS. BENSON
And my other motto is: "Get over yourself!".

THE END

FUNNY SHORTS 2

A KISS IN TIME

FUNNY SHORTS 2

CHARACTERS

PRINCE MAGNUM — A handsome prince in a modern fairy tale. Can be any age from 25-50. Vain, self-centered, a bit dim.

PATSY/LUCY — Sidekick to the prince. In her 20s. Is dressed as a man but does not act overly masculine. The audience knows she is a woman but the prince doesn't. She should have moderately long hair that she hides under a hat or cap.

BEAUTIFUL PRINCESS — Any age up to mid-30s.

FUNNY SHORTS 2

SETTING

A clearing in a forest.

TIME

Late afternoon.

Note:

The actor playing Prince Magnum can have fun by constantly mispronouncing Patsy's name (e.g., Pasty, Pasta, Pastina, Pasta Fazool, etc. Or, just stick to Pasty).

At rise, Prince Magnum and Patsy enter the clearing.

PRINCE MAGNUM
Here's a good spot, Pasty! Let's just sit down and rest our feet, shall we? Or, rather, I'll sit down and you can gather firewood, light a fire, and cook some of that 400 pound boar I just killed back there with nothing but my bare hands.

PATSY
It's Patsy, sire.

PRINCE MAGNUM
What's that?

PATSY
My name is Patsy.

FUNNY SHORTS 2

PRINCE MAGNUM
Let's not quibble, Pasty. You know I have dyslexia, and there's no need to get all excited about a few mixed up letters in a name. Now go ahead man, and find some firewood, will you?

PATSY
Yes, sir. I'm hungry myself, so a meal sounds good.

PRINCE MAGNUM
Yes, well, there may be a few scraps left for you, Pasty, after I've eaten. I'll have to see just how much of an appetite I have. But, you're a scrawny little fellow, so I'm sure it won't be a problem for you to go hungry again.

PATSY
No sire.

PRINCE MAGNUM
I need plenty of protein to keep this body running tiptop! After all, there are dragons to slay, witches to kill, and princesses to kiss, and I'm the only man around who can do it!

PATSY
Yes sire. I'll go get the wood for the fire.

FUNNY SHORTS 2

PRINCE MAGNUM

Good plan! I'll amuse myself by shooting a few birds while I wait. There's nothing like killing small animals to pass the time, I always say!

PATSY

Patsy goes off, stops, sees a girl sleeping

Sire, come quick! I've found something!

PRINCE MAGNUM

What is it? A dragon? A hideous mountain troll? An ugly old witch who has a grudge against handsome princes like me?

PATSY

No, sire, look! It's a sleeping princess!

PRINCE MAGNUM

Oh that? From your tone of voice, I thought you had found something special. There's nothing special about a sleeping princess. You know we come across them all the time, Pasty. Why, she's the third one we've seen this week!

PATSY

Yes, but she's an especially pretty one, don't you think?

FUNNY SHORTS 2

PRINCE MAGNUM
Eh, she's all right. I've seen so many beautiful princesses, they all look the same to me these days.

PATSY
Oh, I think she's a rare one, sire. She looks like an angel to me.

PRINCE MAGNUM
Ha, ha, Pasty, you've always had the worst taste! You wouldn't know a beautiful princess if you fell over one! She's just a run of the mill princess who's been put under a spell by a witch, and she needs a handsome prince like me to kiss her and break the spell. The witches certainly have been active in this kingdom, I'll say that. I'm getting tired of kissing all these princesses and waking them up. It's really been a chore lately.

PATSY
Yes, sire. Well, I guess you should get down to business and kiss her.

PRINCE MAGNUM
I'm not sure I want to. I told you, I'm getting tired of this. I mean, how much do they expect from me? The workload is getting a bit much lately, don't you think?

PATSY

Kissing beautiful princesses, sire? Is that what you mean by workload?

PRINCE MAGNUM

Exactly! My lips are getting chapped from all this kissing, and besides, I used up all my lip balm. Believe me, it takes effort to pucker up all the time — my facial muscles are exhausted. And then of course, they all wake up and want to marry me — I know, I know, you can't blame them, can you? But it always gets awkward after the kissing when they're clinging to me, telling me how beautiful I am, that sort of thing. No, Pasty, it's really a hardship, kissing all these princesses.

PATSY

I see, sire. Well, if it's any consolation, most men would be happy to kiss a beautiful woman like her. They wouldn't consider it work. They would be honored to bestow a kiss on such a beautiful, lovely, angelic—

PRINCE MAGNUM

Pasty, you know I'm not like "most men". I'm one of a kind — the handsomest prince who's ever lived! I'm handsome, tall, charming, handsome, strong, fearless, handsome — it's really unfair that I can't kiss myself, when you think about it.

PATSY
Yes, sire. Even so, you should probably get to work and wake up this princess.

PRINCE MAGNUM
Nope. I told you, I'm not in the mood.

PATSY
But sire, we can't let her stay here.

PRINCE MAGNUM
This is really quite an annoying situation. I mean, there's nobody here to applaud, to sing songs while I work, to spread the news about what I did — how can I motivate myself properly if I don't have an audience?

PATSY
I know it's hard, sire, but it's your duty, don't you think?

PRINCE MAGNUM
Sighs

Yes, I guess it is. We all have our burdens in life, and this is mine. All right, then, move aside and let me kiss the lass.

He kisses the princess

There we go. Another fantastic kiss, even with my chapped lips. I should be paid handsomely for my skill, but it's just my way of contributing something to the world, leaving it a little better than how I found it. Now, Pasty, make sure you keep her away from me when she wakes up. I don't want her hanging all over me and wrinkling my clothes. I just got them pressed last week, and—

PATSY
Sire, she's not waking up.

PRINCE MAGNUM
What? That's impossible. Are you sure?

PATSY
Yes, sire. She hasn't moved at all. Not even the tiniest stirring of an eyelid.

PRINCE MAGNUM
What a strange thing! Perhaps she's just a slow waker. Some people need their coffee to really wake up, even after being kissed by a handsome prince.

FUNNY SHORTS 2

PATSY
I don't think that's it, sire. She's not waking at all.

PRINCE MAGNUM
This has never happened before! What could be the reason?

PATSY
I don't know.

PRINCE MAGNUM
Perhaps I just didn't have my heart in it. That's it! My technique was off because I'm not feeling 100 percent. Did you notice anything different about how I kissed her?

PATSY
No, sire—

PRINCE MAGNUM
Well, you wouldn't, Pasty. You have no experience with kissing, so you don't know about the finer points of it. It's a very complex process and you have do it exactly right. I probably just made a small mistake at some point. Here, I'll try it again and this time I'll do it right! Stand aside, my good fellow!

FUNNY SHORTS 2

He kisses the princess again

There! That should do it! I know I did it right this time.

PATSY
She's still asleep.

PRINCE MAGNUM
What? That's ridiculous. I've never heard of such a thing. I refuse to accept this. Stand aside, Pasty!

He kisses her again, several times with more vigor, and ends with a flourish

And there's another, just for good measure! That should definitely do it! No princess on the planet could stay asleep now!

PATSY
No, sire, it still hasn't worked, I'm afraid.

PRINCE MAGNUM
What? I don't know what's going on here, but that's it, I'm finished. This princess is under some kind of weird spell that doesn't respond to my kisses, and I'm not sticking around one minute longer. Come, Pasty, let us go now.

FUNNY SHORTS 2

PATSY
But sire, we can't just leave her here!

PRINCE MAGNUM
Why not? We've done everything we can.

PATSY
There is one other thing.

PRINCE MAGNUM
What's that?

PATSY
I could kiss her, sire.

PRINCE MAGNUM
You? *(He laughs for a long time, till he has to wipe away tears)* Oh, Pasty, I have to thank you for that. I really needed a good laugh, and you certainly gave me one. It's wonderful how good a person can feel after a laugh like that. I'm feeling so refreshed now! Okay, time to move on, Pasty! Let's go.

PATSY
But sire, I'm serious.

PRINCE MAGNUM
Now, now, Pasty, once is enough. I'm not

going to laugh at the same joke twice.

PATSY
I'm not joking. Maybe I could try kissing her.

PRINCE MAGNUM
But Pasty, you're just a, a — well, I don't really know what you are, but you certainly aren't the kind of person who can wake a princess from a sleeping spell. You're not handsome enough, or strong enough, or smart enough, or fearless enough, and, well, you're certainly not manly enough.

PATSY
Yes, but maybe she's a different kind of princess and she needs a different sort of person to wake her.

PRINCE MAGNUM
Oh, Pasty, that's ridiculous. She's not different — all princesses are the same, and they respond in the same way to a handsome prince like me. That's just the facts, my lad. And the fact that she didn't wake just means she's under a different kind of spell, and I am simply not in the mood to stick around and try to figure this one out. I'm on to new adventures!

FUNNY SHORTS 2

PATSY
I really would like to try it, sire.

PRINCE MAGNUM
Ah, my poor, delusional Pasty. Okay, suit yourself. This should be good for a laugh.

PATSY
Thank you sire. Here goes. (*kisses her*)

PRINCE MAGNUM
See, what did I tell you? It didn't work. Okay, Pasty, let's go.

PRINCESS
Wakes up

Where am I? What happened?

PRINCE MAGNUM
He pushes Pasty aside

You were put under a spell by a witch, and this is your lucky day because I happened by, quickly sized up the situation, and decided to kiss you!

PRINCESS
You kissed me?

FUNNY SHORTS 2

PRINCE MAGNUM

Me, in the flesh. You may thank me, but please don't muss my clothes or hair.

PRINCESS

That's strange.

PRINCE MAGNUM

What do you mean "strange"?

PRINCESS

Well, whoever kissed me made my heart beat very, very fast, but looking at you — well, all of a sudden my heart stopped beating so fast.

PRINCE MAGNUM

Okay, we're done here. Pasty, let's go.

PRINCESS

Who are you?

PATSY

I'm Patsy. I'm the sidekick.

PRINCESS

Sidekick?

PATSY

Yes, that's me. I exist to be Prince Magnum's

servant and helper, and to shower him with endless praise.

PRINCESS
My goodness! *(puts a hand to her chest)* Why is my heart beating so fast all of a sudden?

PATSY
I don't know. Maybe —

PRINCESS
She grabs Patsy and kisses him/her

Wow!

PATSY
Wow!

PRINCE MAGNUM
Wow?

PRINCESS
That settles it — you're the one who kissed me!

PATSY
Yes, princess, it was me. But I shouldn't have done it — I'm not a handsome prince — I only did it because I didn't want to leave you alone in the woods.

PRINCESS
Well, I don't want you to leave me alone either. Stay with me — I will take you back to my father the king and introduce you to my family. I would like to spend more time with you. Lots and lots more time!

PATSY
Oh, princess, that's very nice, but I couldn't.

PRINCESS
Why not?

PRINCE MAGNUM
Because he has to come with me! Pasty is my servant!

PATSY
Yes, he's right. Although not about my name. My name is Patsy. And I am not of noble blood.

PRINCESS
Nonsense! I don't care about any of that. Come with me!

PATSY
I can't. There is another reason.

FUNNY SHORTS 2

PRINCE MAGNUM
What he means is that I simply can't do without Pasty. He makes my tea, cleans my sword after I've slaughtered various creatures, cooks my food — what you're asking is totally out of the question. Come, Pasty, let's—

PATSY
Actually, that is not the reason.

PRINCE MAGNUM
Well what is it?

PATSY
I'm not a man.

PRINCE MAGNUM
To the princess

What he means is he's not a handsome man like me.

PATSY
No, I mean I'm not a man. I'm a woman. (*She takes off her cap to reveal her long hair*)

PRINCE MAGNUM
Pasty, I'm shocked. Have you been lying to me?

PATSY

I'm afraid I have. I wanted adventures. I didn't want the life of an ordinary woman, staying at home and making quilts, and cooking dinner, and milking cows, and all that. It was so boring to me! I wanted to be out in the world doing exciting things, and the only way open to me was to disguise myself as a man.

PRINCE MAGNUM

Well, this is quite a perplexing situation! You mean all this time when I thought you were a trusty male sidekick, you were in fact a, a. . . woman?

PATSY

I am truly sorry, sire. I'm not sorry for wanting something different. I just couldn't live the life that was expected of me, you see. I'm sorry I deceived you, though.

PRINCE MAGNUM

Pasty, you will have to come with me at once back to civilization and receive your punishment, and then you will have to marry and live the life of every woman in the kingdom. There is no choice in this matter! We all have to play the roles that were assigned to us. I mean, what would happen if I suddenly decided I didn't want to play my role anymore? Why, there'd be chaos! Think of all the sleeping princesses out there who would never wake up! And the dragons who wouldn't be slain! Not to mention all the young ladies who would never have the thrill of seeing me in person. It's horrible to think of! Don't you agree, princess?

PRINCESS
Looking at Pasty

Boy, talk about a revelation!

PATSY
I am sorry, princess.

PRINCESS
No, don't be. I always wondered why I was never attracted to all the handsome suitors I had. I was bored with their stories of killing dragons, and to be honest, if I saw one more prince flexing his biceps, I was going to be seriously ill. And yet I was always happy around women. It was very puzzling, and you can't be puzzled when you're a princess, you have to know exactly who you are, so I paid a witch to make a potion that would straighten things out for me. Instead, she must have mixed a potion that put

me to sleep and made it so I could only be awakened by my soulmate — you!

PRINCE MAGNUM
Ha, ha, that's clearly impossible. Princesses don't like other women in that way. They like handsome men like me.

PRINCESS
Not this princess.

PATSY
Are you sure, princess?

PRINCESS
No. I need to try one more time. *(She kisses Patsy again)*

I'm sure now!

PATSY
So am I!

PRINCESS
Come with me to the castle and we'll tell my family. I'm sure they will accept you.

PATSY
You are?

PRINCESS
Well, almost. It takes them a little while to get used to new ideas, actually. I only recently got them to stop burning peasants at the stake when there's a bad harvest. But they're not such a bad lot, and I'm sure in time they'll accept us. It will be an adventure! Are you ready?

PATSY
Yes!

PRINCESS
Oh, just one thing: I don't like the name Patsy. Can I call you Lucia instead? It means Light.

PATSY
I like that name. Yes!

PRINCESS
Good. Let's go!

They exit, arm in arm

PRINCE MAGNUM
Watches them for a beat

It doesn't make sense — what could be the problem here? No, it just doesn't add up. Wait,

I have it! This must be an enchanted forest. Why of course, that's it! They're under an enchantment! All I have to do is find my way out of this forest and everything will be normal again. Oh, good, I'm glad I figured that out. I feel much better now. Now, which way takes me out of this forest?

THE END

FUNNY SHORTS 2

ARE YOU HAPPY?

FUNNY SHORTS 2

CHARACTERS

JOE	Fiftyish, dressed casually. A customer at the Cheerful Store.
MOLLY	A clerk at the Cheerful Store. In her twenties, with an upbeat personality. Very anxious to please her customers.
MARISSA	The manager at the Cheerful Store. Thirtyish. Also very upbeat and determined to please.
FRED	A customer in line behind Joe. Can be any age.
LARRY	Another customer in line behind Joe. Can be any age.

FUNNY SHORTS 2

SETTING

A checkout line at the Cheerful Store.

TIME

Middle of the day, present.

Molly is standing at a counter, and Joe walks up with a bag of potato chips. During the scene, Fred and Larry arrive, and stand in line behind Joe. Toward the end they become increasingly impatient.

MOLLY
Hello, sir, it's a beautiful day, isn't it?

JOE
But it's raining out there.

MOLLY
I know, but the rain is so beautiful! It's like tears of joy falling from the sky.

JOE
I don't care for it myself.

MOLLY
Then I wish I could change it for you and make it a sunny day! We always try to make our customers happy.

JOE
Chuckling

That's very nice, but you can't change the weather.

MOLLY
Well, our Customer Satisfaction department is working on it! Just give us a little time, and we'll have it fixed, I guarantee you!

JOE
Right. I'll just pay for this now, if you don't mind.

MOLLY
Of course! Did you find everything you wanted?

JOE
Yes I did.

MOLLY
There wasn't anything else? Something you couldn't find in the store?

JOE
No, I only needed this bag of potato chips.

MOLLY
Good, because we want our customers to be really happy. Are you really happy?

JOE
Yes, I am. Now if I could just pay—

MOLLY
Of course, I'll ring everything up. Oh, sir, did you know we're having a two for one sale on these potato chips? You could save money!

JOE
No, that's okay. I only need one bag of them.

MOLLY
But sir, we want to help you save money! Why don't you just go back and get another bag?

JOE
No, that's perfectly fine. I live alone, and I don't need more than one.

MOLLY
Oh, I see. (*Touches his arm*). I'm sorry you live alone.

JOE
What? Oh, it's not a problem. I'm fine with it.

FUNNY SHORTS 2

MOLLY
What a brave face you're putting on!

JOE
No, no, I'm fine with it. It's no problem at all.

MOLLY
Yes, I'm sure you tell yourself that when you're sitting alone on your couch eating potato chips and crying softly as you watch the latest Hallmark Christmas special.

JOE
What? I don't sit on my couch and — can you please just tell me what I owe?

MOLLY
Yes, of course. I'll scan these products right away, so you can go home to your stark, desolate, lonely apartment and —

JOE
Could you please stop that? What's the matter with you?

MOLLY
It's against our company policy for our customers to be sad.

JOE
I'm not sad!

MOLLY
Is there no one you could invite over to share your potato chips? Your next-door neighbor? A classmate from your old school? Your local Fed Ex driver? It's terrible the way your family has abandoned you.

JOE
For your information, my family hasn't abandoned me. I have a sister who lives in California, but — hey, do you mind?

MOLLY
Oh, California is so far away! It must be hard to have family living so far away. Do you miss her?

JOE
If you don't stop this I'm going to report you to the manager!

MOLLY
That's a wonderful idea! My manager is a whiz at helping lonely customers like you. She always finds the perfect solution! Just a second while I call her.

JOE
No, don't do that! I changed my mind. Really, you don't need to--

MOLLY
Manager to the front of the store please! We have a depressed customer!

MARISSA
Enters

Hello, it's a beautiful day isn't it? What seems to be the problem?

MOLLY
This poor gentleman lives alone, and he just bought some potato chips to eat on his couch while he cries bitter tears about his loneliness.

MARISSA
Oh, that's terrible! At Cheerful Stores we hate to see that! We need to do something for him! Sir, could we have a group of carolers visit you to sing Christmas carols? Our Maintenance Department is known for their five part harmonies. I'm sure they'll put you in the holiday spirit, and make you forget all about your loneliness.

JOE

Holiday spirit? What are you talking about? It's the end of March!

MARISSA

Yes, but there's nothing like Christmas carols to make you forget you're alone in the world, with not a soul on the planet to share your potato chips with.

JOE

Listen, as I've told your cashier here multiple times, I am NOT lonely! Do you understand? Not lonely! Perfectly happy! Happy as a man can be, that's me! Now will you stop bothering me about that?

MOLLY

To Marissa

He hides it well, doesn't he?

MARISSA

Yes, poor dear. He doesn't want anyone to know.

MOLLY

I have a great idea! How about if I go to his apartment for dinner?

MARISSA
Why, that's perfect! We're not too busy tonight, so I could spare you. Sir, Molly here would like to come to dinner at your apartment.

MOLLY
I could bring a bottle of wine from the back. I'm a good conversationalist, and I would be great company. By the way, do you like white or red? We have a nice selection of cabs, chardonnays, merlots, you name it.

JOE
No, no, no! I don't need to have anyone for dinner. How many times do I have to tell you, I'm perfectly happy eating alone!

MOLLY
It would make me personally very happy to serve you. Plus, I would get a gold star from my boss and I'd be in the running for employee of the month. I won two months in a row, but my co-worker Callie broke my record with three months, because she's been on a hot streak — she cured six different customers of their depression last month alone!

FUNNY SHORTS 2

MARISSA

Callie's a rising star in the company.

JOE

This is absurd! What universe am I in here?

FRED
Behind JOE in line

Hey, buddy, could you move it along?

JOE

I'm trying to get her to hurry up! What do you want me to do?

FRED

Let her come to dinner.

JOE

What? Are you crazy?

FRED

No, it's the only way. This store is famous for its focus on customer satisfaction. They really go out of their way.

LARRY
Behind Fred

Yeah, you should have seen what they did for

my brother and his wife. Paid off their mortgage, built an addition on their house, cured their teenager's acne — unbelievable!

FRED
It's why I come back all the time.

MARISSA
Thank you all — we love to hear that at Cheerful Stores.

JOE
But you can't seriously expect me to—

FRED
Just say yes, will you?

LARRY
Yeah, we can't wait around here forever.

JOE
I give up. Okay, fine, you can come to dinner.

MOLLY
Wonderful! I'm so glad you're letting me serve you this way.

FRED & LARRY
All right! *(they applaud)*

JOE
I can't believe this.

MOLLY
We aim for happiness at Cheerful Stores! Are you happy?

JOE
Yes, yes, yes I'm happy!

MARISSA
Is there anything else we can do for you?

JOE
No, you've done enough!

MOLLY
Good. Just remember to give me a good rating when they call you for the customer survey. It's very important.

MARISSA
Yes, just between you and me, sir, it has a lot to do with Molly's future.

JOE
Her future with the company?

MARISSA
No, her future on this planet. Employees with bad ratings often disappear.

                    JOE
Oh, I see. Well, yes, I'll give her a good review, don't worry!

                    MOLLY
A good review, sir? Is that all?

                    JOE
No, an excellent review! I'll give her a super duper five star review! Is that good enough?

                    MARISSA
Wonderful!

                    MOLLY
I'm eternally indebted to you, sir.

                    JOE
No problem. Can I go now?

            Finishes scanning the potato chips

There you are, sir. It's only $100 for your potato chips.

                    JOE
A hundred dollars? For a bag of potato chips? You can't seriously—

FUNNY SHORTS 2

FRED
Buddy, will you just pay the bill? We can't wait here all day.

MOLLY
If you think I overcharged you, you can certainly give me a lower rating. I'll have to take a 75 percent pay cut and have all my fingers broken, but at least I'll still be alive.

MARISSA
Our goal is five stars from every customer!

JOE
No, no, no! That's not necessary. Here's my credit card – I just want to be done with this.

MOLLY
Swipes it and hands it back

Thank you sir! There you go.

JOE
Please, can I go now? Please?

MOLLY
Of course! I'll be over at six with a bottle of wine and I'll make a steak dinner for you. Will that be satisfactory?

FUNNY SHORTS 2

FRED & LARRY
Say yes! Please say yes!

JOE
Yes, yes, a thousand times yes! Now let me out of here!

Runs off

MOLLY
There goes a happy customer!

MARISSA
And he hasn't even heard about our rewards program! Wait till he finds out about that!

THE END

FUNNY SHORTS 2

GAME THEORY

FUNNY SHORTS 2

CHARACTERS

JOSH Thirtyish. Lives at home with his mother. Is a big video gamer.

VERA Josh's mother. Age 55-65. Very perky and cheerful.

FUNNY SHORTS 2

SETTING

Josh's bedroom. He is playing a video game during the scene, and he talks to the screen at various times, and reacts to the action on his screen. He doesn't take his eyes off the game, even when he's answering Vera.

TIME

Afternoon, present.

FUNNY SHORTS 2

At rise, Josh is seated, playing a video game. Vera walks in. Josh looks at the screen while he talks to her.

JOSH
Mom, what are you doing in my room?

VERA
Oh, just checking Josh. Did you apply for any of those jobs yet?

JOSH
I can't right now, I'm busy.

VERA
Busy?

JOSH
Yes, busy. Can't you see that? I'm already on the second level of this game.

VERA
Laughing, pretending to be stern with him

I see a 30 year old who's playing video games. That's the wrong kind of busyness, young man.

JOSH
Your definition of busy is different than mine. And will you stop straightening up my room?

VERA
It's a mess in here. I'm just trying to put things in order.

JOSH
I like things the way they are.

VERA
You'll have less stress if you arrange things neatly in here.

JOSH
I don't have any stress.

Talking to the screen

Oh my god, there's one behind the bushes! Take that! Whew, that was close.

VERA
Your snow globe collection, for instance. You have them all over the room. They should be put in chronological order. You could put them in a nice straight line according to when your father bought each one.

JOSH

Mom, that's weird. Look, do you mind? I HAVE to finish this game.

VERA

When things are in order, the world is a happier place!

JOSH

Not for me. My handle is the Grim Reaper!

To the screen

I unleash destruction, baby!

VERA

Picks up a snow globe

Aw, do you remember this one? That's the first one your father bought you. He was on a trip to New York and got this at the Empire State building.

JOSH

Yeah, one of his business trips, right? I figured that one out after a while.

To the screen

Can't fool me, you evil Nazi devil! Pow!

FUNNY SHORTS 2

VERA

Puts the first snow globe down and picks up another one

It's amazing how popular snow globes are. And here's one he bought when you were twelve. Remember this? It has the hula girls from Hawaii. Although it doesn't snow in Hawaii, so that was always a little puzzling.

JOSH

He was there with his girlfriend.

VERA

I believe he was there on business, dear.

JOSH

Dream on, Mom. Wow, I just got another one!

To the screen

Can't fool the Grim Reaper, you losers!

VERA

Puts the snow globe down and picks up another one

Oh, and here's the one he got in Quebec, during the winter festival. Look at all that snow!

JOSH
It's not real snow.

VERA
I know that. But it's nice to pretend. What if we lived in a snow globe? Wouldn't that be fun!

JOSH
Pow, bam! The bodies are piling up! I'm really on my game today!

VERA
Of course it would be very claustrophobic inside a snow globe. We all need space, don't we? That's why cities have parks in them. We need open space in our lives, not borders. Even you, you need space, Josh, don't you? I bet you have a secret need to get a job and move out, to finally break out of the prison of your life, right? I'll bet you want to travel and see the world! I'm sure that's what you want to do, am I right?

JOSH
Where I live is not important. Scientists think we're living inside a computer simulation anyway.

VERA
Oh, that's ridiculous.

JOSH
How would we know the difference? It could be like The Matrix, where we're all just lying in vats of chemicals in a warehouse but our brains are connected to a computer program that convinces us we're living in this world. How do you know you're not living in the middle of a computer program? Wow, Level Five! I'm killing it today!

VERA
There's no computer program that could fool me, Josh. I know what's real and what isn't. For example, there's no computer that could come up with the concept of a special friendship. Don't you agree?

JOSH
What are you talking about?

To the screen

Pow! Gotcha!

VERA
I'm talking about the wonderful feeling I get

when I meet Mr. Bannister at that new wine bar in town every time his wife is away on business. Oh, it's just exquisite to sit there and talk about our lives over a glass of Chardonnay! About all our hopes and dreams for the future, plus of course naughty things we'd like to do to after his wife passes away — it's such a lovely feeling to do something illicit like that. It's much more interesting than anything a boring old computer could think up.

JOSH

Mom, sometimes I don't understand how we're related. Uh oh, this is getting scary now. Gotta be real careful...

VERA

Oh, it's really very simple dear. Your father and I—

JOSH

No, no, I don't want to talk about Dad. I have to focus!

VERA

He would have been very happy with the way you turned out, I just know it. Your father was quite an adventurous soul, wasn't he? Just like you. Well, the difference is your adventures are on a screen, but his were in the real world. And wasn't I happy when he finally took me on one of his trips! Skiing in the Rocky Mountains! Of course, it was such a tragedy when he fell off that cliff when nobody was around us. I bet a computer couldn't think up that scenario!

JOSH

What? Listen Mom, I really need to concentrate now. I've never made it to this level before. Do you mind?

VERA

You know, I just had the cutest idea for a snow globe. It could be a mountain with snow all over it, and at the bottom there's a big pile of snow with a pair of skis peeking out of it. And some blood on the snow too. Wouldn't that be adorable?

JOSH

Mom, please! This is getting really intense.

VERA

Alright, I'll go. But promise me you'll stop soon.

JOSH

Mom!

VERA

Okay, dear. Enjoy your game!

She starts to walk out then turns.

VERA

Honey, I forgot to tell you. I'll be gone next week for a few days. Mr. Bannister and I are taking his wife on a ski trip!

JOSH

Annoyed

Mom! You broke my concentration and I just got killed! Thanks a lot!

VERA

Oh, I'm sorry. But it's better anyway. You shouldn't be playing so many video games, dear. I don't want you to lose touch with reality.

THE END

LESS IS MORE

FUNNY SHORTS 2

CHARACTERS

EDWARD MORRIS   Mid to late 40s. An executive at a large art museum. Is wearing a blazer, tie, crisp shirt and pants.

ZINA NULL   Late 20s. An up and comer in the museum field. Committed to minimalism in every aspect of her life. Wearing all black.

SETTING

Edward's office at the museum. He is sitting at his desk. He has various objects on the desk – a notebook, a computer, a picture of his wife, pen, etc.

TIME

Present. Mid-afternoon.

Note: The actor playing Zina is free to gradually move around more as the play progresses, straightening the papers on Edward's desk, his tie, moving his desk while he's talking, etc.

At rise, Edward is sitting at his desk, and Zina enters. She is carrying a cardboard box, which she puts on the floor when she sits down.

ZINA
Mr. Morris?

EDWARD
Zina Null? Come in, come in. Nice to meet you. I'm so excited to finally meet you. Sit down!

ZINA
Yes.

EDWARD
I see you've brought a box with you.

ZINA
Yes.

EDWARD
I'm just curious why you'd —

ZINA
It's important.

EDWARD
Oh, right! Yes, well, I suppose you have your reasons.

ZINA
Yes. I do.

EDWARD
Well, before we get started with the interview, would you like a coffee?

ZINA
No.

EDWARD
Tea?

ZINA
No.

EDWARD
Water, then?

ZINA
No.

EDWARD
I see. Fine, fine. You're known as somebody who doesn't like to waste time, so we'll just get started on the interview.

ZINA
Excuse me.

She reaches over and straightens a pile of papers on the desk

EDWARD
Oh, thank you. Yes, I've been meaning straighten up that pile of papers. Thank you very much. Now, I just want to say I am SO impressed by your qualifications. Art education from the best schools, internships with leading museums, plus a pioneering record as an administrator at the Minimalist wing of the museum of modern art.

ZINA
Yes.

EDWARD
Right. As I understand it, you're the actual person who came up with the idea of minimalism. Is that correct?

ZINA

Yes.

EDWARD

Reads from a paper on his desk

That's so impressive! I did quite a bit of research on you, and it says here that you became disenchanted with all the noise and distraction of modern life, and you thought we needed to get back to a simpler way of living, a time before the frenzy and madness of our world today. Am I quoting you correctly?

ZINA

She nods yes

EDWARD

It's quite a radical idea, of course, but you certainly hit on something that resonates with lots of people. Lots and lots of people. Me too, as a matter of fact. Oh, yes, I really think you've hit on something. Life is just too cluttered these days, way too cluttered, if you ask me.

ZINA

She reaches over and straightens his tie.

EDWARD
Nervous laugh

Oh, thank you. As I was saying, I agree so much with what you're saying. There's so much distraction in our lives, it's like we all have attention deficit disorder, we're just crying out for a simpler, neater, more ordered life. I suppose that's your whole idea in a nutshell, right?

ZINA
She nods yes

EDWARD
Good, good. Well, let's move on to some of the highlights of your resume. You've had a very successful career, it seems. Some of the exhibitions you put on, just fantastic! So radical, so avant grade, eh? Like the one where you had a room full of blank canvases, that was very good.

ZINA
She nods yes

EDWARD
Brilliant, just brilliant! And the one where you had an exhibit of the work of famous writers who

suffered from writer's block, with page after page of blank paper covering the walls of a room— the Times called it "a masterful rendering of the angst of the modern writer." Groundbreaking! How did you come up with that idea?

ZINA
She shrugs as if to say, "I don't know".

EDWARD
Right! And the piece de resistance, the one where there was just an empty room with a glass case, complete with a rope line and armed security guards to manage the crowds of people. They would let one person in at a time to look at the empty glass case —genius! You really outdid yourself on that one, didn't you? It was celebrated as the art exhibition of the decade! What were your thoughts as you assembled that exhibit?

ZINA
She shrugs again.

EDWARD
Getting nervous, and talking more

I see! Well, all I can say is we love your style, and

that's why we called you in. Frankly, this museum has been here for over 100 years, and it's gotten somewhat stodgy lately. Oh, sure, we have some of the premier works of art of the world here, no doubt about it, but we could use some new ideas, a fresh look at how to present these works, and we think you're the person who could do it. Now, for instance, what would you do for our world-famous Picasso collection?

ZINA

Garbage.

EDWARD

Excuse me? Did you just say garbage?

ZINA

She nods yes.

EDWARD

But people love Picasso! He's one of the great figures of Western Art, of course, and that exhibit really brings in the crowds—

ZINA

Too many lines.

EDWARD

Too many lines of people to see the paintings?

Well, yes, I know, but all those people bring in a lot of money for the museum, and—

ZINA

Too many lines IN the paintings.

EDWARD

Too many lines in — oh! Picasso has too many lines in his paintings! Now I get it. What genius! That's quite an insight! Wow, you really are good. I'm not sure how our board will respond to that idea, of course, but I think I see what you're getting at. Okay, then, let's try another question. What would you do about our Michelangelo sculpture, the companion to the David in Florence?

ZINA

Smash.

EDWARD

Yes, it is a smash hit with our patrons. They absolutely love that Michelangelo!

ZINA

Shakes her head no.

EDWARD

What? You can't mean smash, as in smash up

the sculpture. You don't mean that, do you?

Beat

Do you?

ZINA
Shakes her head yes.

EDWARD
The Michelangelo? But it's a priceless treasure! It's unique! Why would you do something like that?

ZINA
Too much stone.

Zina finds a broom and starts sweeping the floor behind Edward. Gets a dustpan and brush and sweeps up the pile, then empties it offstage, all while Edward is talking.

EDWARD
Too much stone. Too much stone. Hmm. Okay. . . well, maybe, maybe. I suppose using all that stone is very wasteful, and, and not good for the environment somehow. I guess we could support that – maybe use the stone to make something useful for poor people.

Ahem, let's move on then. How about our Impressionist section, oh that's a real crowd pleaser! The Renoirs, the Monets, the Manets — folks just love them.

ZINA

Too many colors.

EDWARD

Too. Many. Colors? Is that what you—

ZINA

Nods yes

EDWARD

That's, that's. . . brilliant! Yes, that's what it must be. Yes, yes of course! I see what you're doing! You think there's been too much visual extravagance in Western art, too much elitism, too much of the Eurocentric focus, right? Too much, too much. . . something!

ZINA

Shrugs

EDWARD

You're saying that we need to exhibit art works that are truly radical, truly groundbreaking, that truly speak to the bare facts of existence, that really get down to the bone without all the frills and extravagances of modern capitalist culture. It's the truth of existence you're after, the real nitty gritty, the nuts and bolts, the foundational truths of art. Yes, yes, I see! That's what you're saying, right?

ZINA

Shrugs

EDWARD

Of course, of course, yes indeed. You're rejecting art that is too, too, visual, too artistic, too thingy! Yes, you're rejecting the idea of art as a thing, as something that exists. It's so radical! We are seduced by the visual qualities of art, and we need to get back to the power of, of. . .nothingness! That's it, absolute nothingness is the one quality we should celebrate in art! Nothing is the highest form of art! Nothing IS art! Nothing is everything! That's what you're getting at, right? Art that's a big fat zero, right?

ZINA

Bends down to tie his shoe

EDWARD

What are you doing? Oh, thank you, that's

very nice. Well, all I can say is this brilliant! Just brilliant! I want to offer you the job right now. You're just what this museum needs. We'll go in a new direction, clear out the old cobwebs, start fresh, forge a new path to a brave new world of art and life! It's brilliant, it's masterful, it's — what are you doing?

ZINA
She starts putting things from his desk into the box: his pen, his phone, a brown paper bag with his lunch, and a picture of his wife.

EDWARD
But that's my favorite pen! And that's my phone! And that's my lunch! And that's, that's my picture of my wife!

ZINA
Keeps putting things from the desk into the box, then gives him the box and pushes him out as he keeps talking.

EDWARD
Oh, I see, I see. Yes, I have it — we all need to pare down our lives. There's too much clutter! Yes, it's the dilemma of modern life — all these things and people that are simply weighing us

down! This is genius! You're telling us to eliminate the unnecessary from our lives!

Zina walks back onstage and looks around the office, then Edward comes back, talking all the while.

EDWARD
Masterful! To get right down to what's important, to get rid of the junk, the clutter, the debris of modern life. Even the relationships that weigh us down! This is really a life-changing moment for me. I'm so glad I called you in, I am so grateful that I've found someone who has such an understanding of modern life, and is leading the way toward Truth, toward Absolute Minimalism...

ZINA
She escorts him out again and he's talking nonstop as he exits, saying, "Eliminate the unnecessary! Get rid of the excess!" Then she comes back and sits down, turns to the audience and smiles.

EDWARD
Offstage

Brilliant! Get rid of the clutter! It's genius,

that's what it is!

THE END

HOW TO SPOT A ZOMBIE

CHARACTERS

AMY   Mid-30s. Businesslike. Wearing a dark suit.

BILL   Late 50s or older. Dressed casually.

FUNNY SHORTS 2

SETTING

A room in a funeral home, before a funeral service. Folding chairs are set up. The coffin is not visible, and the actors are facing the audience. The coffin is understood to be in the direction of the audience.

TIME

Mid-morning.

Amy is sitting in a chair. Bill enters and sits next to her.

BILL
Well, I guess it's just you and me here, right?

AMY
Yes, I suppose so.

BILL
It's a shame when a funeral service is poorly attended, don't you think?

AMY
Yes it is.

BILL
Family?

AMY
What?

BILL
Are you family? Related to the deceased?

AMY
No.

BILL
Oh then you're a friend?

AMY
Me? Oh, I'm just. . . er, who did you say you were?

BILL
Looks around, then whispers

I don't usually tell people, but since there's nobody else here — I'm a hobbyist.

AMY
A what?

BILL
A funeral hobbyist. Attending funerals is a hobby of mine.

AMY
Are you serious?

BILL
Oh, yes. I've been doing it for years now. I look up funerals in the obituaries and I attend them. I come to the viewing, make small talk, attend the service, sing a few hymns if I know the words, that type of thing. I've developed

my own rating system for funerals. Most of them are just three or four stars, but I have been to a few five star ones.

AMY

You're kidding.

BILL

No, no, I take my funerals seriously. The ones like this, of course, that are poorly attended, I don't rate them. I consider this my pro bono work.

AMY

Pro bono?

BILL

For free. A small funeral like this, there's no chance I'll get invited to the luncheon. I just do it out of the goodness of my heart.

AMY

You go to luncheons when you don't know the deceased person?

BILL

Sure. The larger funerals, you know, it's easy to fall through the cracks. Everybody thinks I'm a distant relative, a long lost cousin, that type of thing. And of course, I research the deceased on the Internet so I know a few facts to throw out if anyone starts talking to me. I tell them about what a great guy Harry was in the Army, or maybe how we were fraternity brothers in college — that kind of thing.

AMY
That's a little dishonest, isn't it?

BILL
But it's a great hobby — you meet the most interesting people — and let me tell you, I have had some lunches to die for – sorry about the pun, it's important to have a sense of humor in this hobby. Anyway, it keeps me busy. I used to go to funerals part time, but I got laid off from my job recently, so I have more free time now. But how about you? Did you say you're a friend of the deceased?

AMY
No, uh. Not a friend.

BILL
But you said you're not family, right?

AMY
No, not family.

BILL

I see. Then you must have had a forbidden love affair.

AMY

What?

BILL

A dark, passionate affair that had to be kept secret for many, many years, and now it's finally coming to light at the funeral. It's okay, you can tell me — we're the only people here, after all.

AMY

Absolutely not! Why would you think that?

BILL

Listen, when you've been to as many funerals as me, you see some crazy stuff. You wouldn't believe who shows up at these things. I've seen fistfights break out in front of the coffin, guns pulled — you name it.

AMY

Well, I'm not a forbidden lover. I worked with him, that's all. Just a casual work acquaintance.

BILL
Oh, that's nice. How long did you work with him?

AMY
Only a year or so.

BILL
Which company was that?

AMY
It was the one that he worked at last. The manufacturing company.

BILL
Right, the manufacturing company. What was the name again?

AMY
Uh, it was, um. . . I don't recall.

BILL
You don't remember the name of the company? I thought you worked there.

AMY
Only for a few months, and it was a long time ago.

BILL
I thought you said it was the deceased's last job.

AMY
Yes, but that was so many years ago. He's been retired for so many —

BILL
The obituary said he was only retired a year when he died.

AMY
Right, right. What was that name? Uh, the ABC Company, that was it!

BILL
Wrong. It was the XYZ Company. You didn't know him at all, did you?

AMY
Hey, I resent that. You think I would lie about something like that?

BILL
I certainly do. Because you, my friend, are a funeral hobbyist just like me.

AMY
What are you talking about?

BILL

I recognize a fellow hobbyist when I see one. So you're the new gal in town, I take it? You moving in on my turf?

AMY

It's a free country. I can do what I want.

BILL

Not in my town. I've been working this turf for years, and it's mine. You just back off, you hear? This town ain't big enough for two funeral hobbyists.

AMY

You're pretty territorial, aren't you? Listen, one thing about funerals: they're not going away. There's plenty of 'em around for us to share.

BILL

No dice. I'm not interested. The next funeral I see you at, you're going to regret it. You've been warned.

AMY

I'm sorry you feel that way. I guess I'll have to come clean with you then.

BILL
What do you mean?

AMY
I'm not a funeral hobbyist, I'm a zombie spotter.

BILL
What the hell is a zombie spotter?

AMY
Shows her ID card

Here's my ID. I'm with Homeland Security, Anti-Zombie Department. Our job is to attend funerals of people we suspect of being infected by zombies. We have to verify that they're really dead. So we come to the funerals to make sure they don't suddenly open their eyes and try to climb out of the coffin. I've got a flamethrower to finish them off if that happens.

BILL
A flamethrower? Here?

AMY
It's in my car. Zombies don't move very fast, so there's plenty of time for me to grab the

flamethrower, get back inside, and fry them to a crisp.

BILL

That's absurd. There's no such thing as zombies.

AMY

Well of course you'd think that. It means we're doing our job well, doesn't it?

BILL

Look, don't give me that BS. I go to funerals all the time and I've never seen anybody open their eyes and climb out of a coffin.

AMY

That's because this town has been zombie free for many years. But there's been an outbreak just across the state line, and my boss is afraid it might spread here. I'm on the lookout for any signs.

BILL

You can't be serious.

AMY

I'm deadly serious. I just showed you my ID, didn't I?

BILL

Yeah, I admit it looks official. Geez, what a crazy world we live in.

AMY

Tell me about it.

BILL

So how long you been doing this job?

AMY

Proudly

This is actually my first assignment!

BILL

Really? They let rookies do this kind of work?

AMY

I'm not a rookie, I've been with the department for a while. I got promoted because I was on a SWAT team that exterminated a vampire in Perkinsville, and they said I did such a good job I deserved a promotion. I went up two pay grades!

BILL

Good for you.

AMY
Thanks. I'm happy with my career progress so far. You know, you should look into this. We're hiring right now, and you'd make a great zombie spotter.

BILL
I don't know.

AMY
No, you'd be great at it. You have all this experience attending funerals. You know what someone looks like when they're really dead — you'd be perfect. With this outbreak almost on our doorstep, we need more boots on the ground in this town. The feds just increased our hiring budget, so we're looking for new bodies. In a manner of speaking.

BILL
But I don't know how use a flamethrower.

AMY
A couple of lessons and you'll be fine. And besides, the benefits in this job are awesome. Three weeks paid vacation, ten sick days, full health care — you can't beat it. The only problem is if you get bit by a zombie. The health care plan doesn't apply

to the undead. Other than that, it's a sweet deal!

BILL
It sounds pretty good. I'll think about it.

AMY
You should.

BILL
Okay. Well, I have to be going. I have two more funerals today.

AMY
Good. Well I might see you at them. The O'Reilly and Santini ones, right?

BILL
Yep.

AMY
They're on my list. I just need to stick around here a few more minutes to make sure he's really dead. If I see any movement in that coffin, I'll have to fry him.

BILL
I understand. See you around?

FUNNY SHORTS 2

                AMY
You bet.

                BILL
Oh, and by the way...

                AMY
Yes?

                BILL
Thank you for your service!

                AMY
No problem. Just doing my part to keep this country zombie free.

                THE END

RECOVERED MEMORY

FUNNY SHORTS 2

CHARACTERS

TED   Mid-60s. Trying to look important at his high school reunion, but is nervous underneath.

DIANE   His wife. Has a wry sense of humor.

SUE   Mid-60s, dressed simply but elegantly. Very sincere.

SETTING

A cocktail party in a hotel ballroom, before dinner.

TIME

Evening. Present.

TED
Why did you talk me into coming to this reunion? I haven't been back in 50 years, how am I supposed to remember these people?

DIANE
I think it's going to be fun. Besides, I'm curious to get an idea of what you were like in high school. You never talk about it.

TED
That's because I've repressed all the memories. I couldn't wait to get out of this town, and I never wanted to come back. I'm a different person, Diane. I'm a successful lawyer, I have respect, I'm a pillar of my community on the coast, which is a universe away from here, and I have no interest in reliving the past. I shouldn't have come, it's just going to be awkward.

DIANE
Awkward? For who? What's the matter, do you have skeletons in your closet? Do you have something to hide, Ted? I bet you had quite a time in high school, didn't you?

TED

I've got nothing to hide. At least, nothing that I remember. It was so long ago, who remembers?

DIANE

I have perfect memories of high school. Maybe that's because my conscience is clear. Is there something you need to tell me?

TED

I had my share of, uh, oh never mind. This conversation is getting ridiculous.

DIANE

Fine. I'm going to get a drink, and I'll get one for you too.

TED

Just hurry up, will you? People are going to come over and start talking to me.

DIANE

Well, you're a big boy. If someone comes over and talks to you, I'm sure you'll be able to handle it. I'll be back in a minute.

She leaves

TED
Wait!

He starts to follow her, then sees a woman walking up to him.

SUE
Teddy? Teddy Brewer? Hi, do you remember me?

TED
Looks for her name tag, but she's not wearing one.

Why of course I do! Yes, yes, yes!

SUE
Oh, good, I didn't know if you would, since I forgot my name tag. You might not recognize me because it's been a long time since graduation.

TED
No, no, I recognize you. Absolutely, are you kidding? Definitely.

SUE
Well, it's been 50 years, and I don't look the same.

TED
You look great. Terrific!

SUE
I know I've changed, you don't have to flatter me.

TED
No, no, I'm telling you, if I didn't know it was 50 years—

SUE
You look great yourself.

TED
Me? Oh, I'm just muddling along. But you! You!

SUE
Well, we're not high schoolers anymore.

TED
No, we're not — ha, ha!

SUE
Those were great days, weren't they?

TED
I'll never forget them. Never, never, never.

FUNNY SHORTS 2

                SUE

Do you remember senior year?

                TED

Do I? I can't forget — it's etched in my mind.

                SUE

That time when we all went to the baseball game?

                TED

The baseball game! Oh, I remember those baseball games.

                SUE

And then the party afterward at Joey's house?

                TED

Ha! The party! Oh, man!

                SUE

His parents weren't home? We all got drunk?

                TED

Oh. Drunk. Right! Sure! What a time that was, huh?

                SUE

And you and me — we went in his parents' bedroom—

FUNNY SHORTS 2

TED

His parents' bedroom! His parents' bedroom. You did say bedroom, right?

SUE

That was quite a night.

TED

Yes, maybe. Of course, my memory is not—

SUE

I really thought I loved you.

TED

No! I mean, yes! Yes, that might be true!

SUE

I never told you, but it was my first time being intimate with a boy.

TED

First time! Your very first time! Wow.

SUE

You really opened my eyes.

TED

Right. I'm glad I could do that. Of course, we were so young, and—

FUNNY SHORTS 2

SUE

I still treasure the memory.

TED

Memories! They're wonderful things. If they're accurate, of course. Sometimes things get mixed up. You can't always trust—

SUE

I never expected there would be consequences.

TED

Did you say consequences? Is that what you said?

SUE

Yes. When you're young you just don't realize how your actions can affect the rest of your life.

TED

Did you know scientists say that our brains are not fully developed till we're 25? In fact, many scientists say it's at least 30! You just can't trust people with undeveloped brains, and--

SUE

Sometimes those decisions you make as a teenager, they really alter your life.

TED

It's kind of warm in here, don't you think? I wonder what happened to the air conditioning.

SUE

One evening in your life, and it just changes everything.

TED

Everything! Wow, I'm really sweating here. Somebody needs to turn on the —

SUE

Your whole life, it just goes in a different direction. It's one of those life-changing things.

TED

Is it hot for you? Maybe the thermostat's broken. I hope I'm not having a heart attack or anything.

SUE

I'm so glad you're here. I've always wanted to tell you about it. Do you know what happened to me as a result of that night?

TED

Multiple personality disorder! Yes, I have

multiple personality disorder. It started in high school. I actually have 25 different personalities, and I never know who's going to show up next. You're actually talking to Alfred, he's a Cockney fishmonger — "'ello, luv, how ya doin'? You're a right fine bird, aren't you?" Alfred, stop it, that's rude. I'm sorry, he has no manners. It's really been a trial for me, and—

SUE
It confirmed that I was gay.

TED
I have NO idea what these personalities will do or— what did you say?

SUE
That one night changed everything. I realized after being with you that I just didn't like men that way. I mean, there was no excitement, no thrill, nothing!

TED
Nothing? Did you say -- nothing?

SUE
Nothing. It confirmed what I was slowly realizing — that I liked women much more. It gave me the

courage to come out as a lesbian when I went off to college, and I never looked back.

                    TED
Oh. Right.

                    SUE
You were the deciding factor. You know, it wasn't easy to come out as gay back then.

                    TED
No. I suppose it wasn't.

                    SUE
It was a very repressive time.

                    TED
Repressive. Yes it was.

                    SUE
But one night with you, and —

                    TED
Right, right, I get it completely.

                    SUE
I've always wanted to thank you for that.

                    TED
No problem. Er, glad I could help.

SUE

Well, I guess I should be going. My wife is here with me, and I'd better go rescue her. She doesn't know anyone, so it's a little hard for her.

TED

Right.

SUE

It was great seeing you.

TED

You too.

SUE

And thanks again.

TED

Oh, please. Not a problem.

SUE

Bye!

TED

Bye.

> *She leaves. Diane comes back from the other direction with two glasses of wine.*

DIANE
Who was that?

TED
Grabs a glass of wine from Diane and drinks it in one gulp

I have no idea. I don't remember her at all. Complete blank, just a blank slate. No memory at all!

DIANE
Are you sure? You seem a bit rattled.

TED
Rattled? I'm not rattled. Listen, do you mind if I have yours also?

Reaches for Diane's glass, but she pulls it away

DIANE
Okay, buddy, let's have the truth. Who is she? An old girlfriend? Or maybe just a one-night stand? Is that it?

TED
It's private, okay? All I'll say is I played a very important role in her life, apparently.

DIANE
Really?

TED
Yes. You could say I helped her make an important decision. See? I wasn't all just about breaking girls' hearts in high school.

DIANE
Well, aren't you the big shot! You had more of an impact in this town than I realized.

TED
I guess I did, now that you put it that way.

DIANE
It's always good to know the history of a great man.

TED
Very funny.

DIANE
So what was it you did for her?

TED
Oh, just forget it. Are you sure you want that wine? Because if you don't, I'm getting another one.

THE END

Did you like this book? I encourage you to write a short review on Amazon. Reader reviews are extremely important in today's publishing world, and I'd be eternally grateful if you'd take the time to write one (no matter what rating you give the book). Thanks!

You can discover more of my books on Amazon

https://www.amazon.com/John-McDonnell/e/B004AXGYHQ/ref=dp_byline_cont_pop_ebooks_1

John McDonnell's Website

https://www.johnfmcdonnell.com

McDonnell Writing Facebook Page

https://www.facebook.com/JohnMcDonnellsWriting

Want to give me your feedback? Send an email: mcdonnellwrite@gmail.com

Printed in Great Britain
by Amazon